WHY WILD EDIBLES?

WHY WILD EDIBLES?

*The Joys of Finding, Fixing, and Tasting
West of the Rockies*

by

RUSS MOHNEY

Published by
PACIFIC SEARCH
715 Harrison Street
Seattle, Washington 98109

Cover and Page Design by Lou Rivera

Copyright © 1975 by Pacific Search
International Standard Book Number 0-914718-07-X
Library of Congress Catalog Card No. 75-12071
Printed in the U.S.A.

DEDICATION

To Janet, an extraordinary wife, who slogged through mud and brambles, watched her kitchen become a shambles of cattails and jelly jars, tasted the dishes, good and bad, and smiled (and maybe fibbed a little); who read the stumbling early passages and lifted the sagging spirits when they fell, gently helping shape the final work, this book is dedicated with love.

ACKNOWLEDGMENTS

The author gratefully acknowledges the contributions made to this work by many people who gave freely of their time and knowledge. Although it is impossible to name them individually, special thanks go to the staff of the Cooperative Extension Service of Washington State University, who helped so much along the way; the staff at the University of Washington Arboretum and Herbarium, who aided in locating many of the rare species in the wild; to many friends of the Quinault Nation, whose knowledge of the plants transcended the generations; to the half dozen professional nutritionists who brought me the bits and pieces that eventually became the whole; officials of the U.S. Department of Agriculture, who generously shared the results of their exhaustive plant investigations and analyses; and to three generations of my own family, who learned—one by one—the demanding lesson of the wilderness, and passed along the joys of a wild harvest!

For reviewing the manuscript and giving valuable criticism and suggestions, I also thank Bea Donovan, Janet Hohn, Cris Trahms, Dr. Melinda Denton, Dr. William S. Chilton, and Dr. John Hill.

PREFACE

A growing number of people are rediscovering their taste buds by finding and using some of the wild plants that grow around them. They are prowling around the ponds and fields for the vegetables that are awaiting to provide the new tastes, natural nutrients, and fun of foraging that were once a way of life for all.

From earliest times until recently, man's first concern has been finding food. Through painful trial and error he learned which things he could eat and which would eat him first. Sometime in the dim past he decided that plants have two distinct advantages over other food: they can't run away and they seldom—if ever—bite back. No wonder the vegetable kingdom supplied much of his food!

Through a great deal of experimentation, man selected about 200 of the safest and easiest plants to include in his everyday diet. At any time of the year some of those were available, they filled his stomach, and they probably tasted at least tolerable, if not downright pleasant.

But man is an adaptable creature who has historically looked for the easy way out. He found that if he collected the seeds of a favorite food and planted them near his shelter, the plants would grow. He had taken the first step to end the ceaseless foraging that had occupied so much of his time. He began cultivating and hybridizing the plants to provide a greater yield with less effort. Finally, the similarities between his plants and those of nature almost disappeared.

As certain cultivated crops became easier to handle, the more difficult ones were dropped from his inventory until only a handful remained. Today, of the thousands of varieties of fruits and vegetables, only a small percentage are widely cultivated for human consumption. They supply necessary nutrients and are conveniently mass-produced at reasonable cost.

With all this development, man forgot what the plants tasted like. The neighborhood supermarket probably has only a dozen or so separate tastes at any one time. When he limited the kind and number of plants he would grow, he also limited the varieties of enjoyment he could get from his food.

In the ensuing years, we have developed seasonings, condiments, blenders, pressure cookers, and a zillion other ways to put more *taste* into the foods we eat. Yet there is a whole world of new and exciting tastes no farther than the nearest woodlot or open space down the block. Most of the plants that were once an important part of life—before the advent of nitrogen fertilizers, mechanical pickers, and quick-freezes—are still thriving in the natural areas of this land.

This book was conceived as an accurate, useful guide to many of the wild edible plants west of the Rockies. It not only identifies the most common and abundant plants, but tells how to prepare them in the field. It also includes many recipes that will enable the collector to make the most of his find.

Highly technical descriptions of the plants are not included. Instead, I have relied on photographs, drawings, and simple descriptions to help you identify each plant and select the edible portion. In most cases a step-by-step description of the actual field preparation is also included so that even the novice collector can handle the plant with no trouble.

Old-timers will recognize many of the plants in this book, while many of their favorites will be missing. It isn't possible to list all of the edible plants that occur west of the Rockies, especially those that are highly regionalized, since this involved more than 2000 species. Instead, I have selected those plants that are among the most common and easily found. Many are distributed throughout the continent; others are more or less limited to the western United States and Canada but are widely found throughout the region. All of the recommended plants included are edible, tested in the laboratory and through historic usage. Those of doubtful value have been excluded or are identifed as being unreliable under certain circumstances. The result is a guide that can be used with confidence in virtually any area or circumstance.

No effort was made to include the plants of arid and desert regions, since they are highly specialized and require special techniques for handling and collecting. There are many edible desert plants, and several excellent guidebooks are available.

There are three groups of plants that I have excluded because of their uncertain reliability. The most prominent of these are the plants that tend to absorb dangerous elements from polluted air and water.

A second group has been shown to absorb quantities of chemicals from agricultural or forest fertilizers and herbicides. The widespread use of these chemicals over the past few decades has rendered some previously edible plants quite harmful.

Finally, most of those plants that have escaped cultivation—the so-called "volunteers"—have been excluded. Several of those have hybridized into varieties that look similar to the domestic plant but contain toxins.

The vast majority of the plants included here are so abundant they are often classified as obnoxious weeds and can be gathered freely without danger to the species. In a few cases, I have listed plants that are rare or endangered. I do not, by any means, advocate the collection of rare edibles. Where such a plant is discussed, it is included for interest or as a survival food, but is not to be gathered from any place where it is scarce.

Although these wild edibles may not become a major part of your diet, they provide an expanded outdoor experience. With this guide in your pack or pocket, get set for some great fun and new horizons.

TABLE OF CONTENTS

COLOR PLATES—PHOTOS BY:

CHAPTER 1
Gathering Wild Edibles

Why Wild Edibles? There are several good reasons for becoming a forager. Probably the most important is for the fun. There is a certain self-sufficiency that comes from being able to partially support yourself in the wilderness. And there are other reasons.

A lot of people gather some wild foods as a matter of economy. A quick trip through the produce department of the local supermarket proves that cultivated vegetables are expensive. They may not be available when you want them, or they may be of poor quality. Many plants from the large growers are picked before they are ripe, and then artificially matured without benefit of the nutrients from sun and soil. Fruit, in particular, is often picked well before it is ready, and I believe the flavor is inferior to vine-ripened fruit. I find it hard to believe that the artificially-ripened fruit can have its full complement of vitamins and minerals.

I am one of those who believe that the nutritional value of the wild plants is higher than that of their domestic counterparts. To me vegetables from a home garden are superior to those produced commercially, and the wild plant is better for being spared the "advantages" of chemical fertilizers and forced growth. Even if the food value is not changed, flavor and appearance seem to suffer from the modern agricultural methods.

Sometimes the only reason for including wild edibles in your diet is the pleasure of experiencing new and different tastes. Anyone who has tasted the tiny scarlet wild strawberry knows that there is no other fruit that can compare with it in flavor. It is impossible to describe the taste, since no cultivated plant (including strawberries) even remotely reminds one of the wild fruit. A fresh-picked cattail shoot somewhat resembles the taste of a cucumber, but the subtle differences in taste and texture cannot be described in mere words. You must taste the cattail shoot to appreciate its gentle flavor. Common dock, a pest in many yards and gardens, is a regular item at my house, simply because we enjoy it and cannot find that flavor elsewhere. True, it slightly resembles asparagus in color and taste, but the *differences* are the reason we like it. Dozens of wild edibles have flavors distinctly their own, incomparable to any in the supermarket.

Finally, they are an important and enjoyable addition to the popular backpacker's foods. After these store-bought foods are frozen, dried, beaten, shaped, chopped, mutilated, folded, and spindled—and had vitamins and minerals pumped in—they are reconstituted with creek water and cooked. In most cases they are pretty good and provide the necessary nutrients, but they often taste a lot like the cardboard box they came in. The additon of a plate of steaming nettle greens or wild onion changes the meal from a routine to a delight.

Some Nutritional Comments: I have attempted to include some nutritional information on the plants described, but that's pretty tough. In most cases, either no extensive research has been done or the results were so widely variable that no absolute conclusions could be drawn. Even in the cases where the plant was the subject of extensive research, the experts don't seem to agree. Many of them contend that soil, sun, and water conditions vary so much from place to place that an analysis on a given plant is not necessarily reliable for a similar plant growing a few miles away. As you discover differences in the appearance of plants growing in various places, you might be persuaded to agree.

Some of the nutritional data were collected to provide information to horticulturists and dairymen, rather than human nutritionists. Although this information is probably pretty reliable, we will doubtless be eating these foods in substantially smaller quantities than the average Guernsey.

In a table, I included the results of detailed analyses of some plants. These figures are intended as a general guide, but won't apply exactly to the plant in question. The tests were almost always made on the cultivated version, which undoubtedly differs from the one you will find out in the brush.

It's a lot more important, at least for our purposes, to know that the plant has been used successfully over the years by others. From their experience, our own boundaries of enjoyment have been greatly expanded. For example, Lewis and Clark used arrowhead as an essential staple during their torturous winter along the Columbia River. In much better times, my friends and I have enjoyed this delectable as a potato substitute at a hearty country breakfast. During the great Depression following the crash of 1929, literally thousands of families revived the old skills of living off the land. The lowly dock became a commonplace green vegetable on the dinner plates of America. Today it is overlooked by most households, but it remains a delicious, nutritious vegetable for anyone who wishes to try it.

After all, this book is intended to be a guide for people who enjoy gathering and eating wild edibles, not a laboratory text for dietitians or food-faddists.

Positive Identification: Always be *absolutely certain* you have correctly identified every plant before you eat it. Unfortunately, a few really deadly plants somewhat resemble others that are quite edible and delicious. Whenever possible, this guide warns of look-alikes. Most edible plants included here were selected partly because they are hard to confuse with dangerous plants that grow in the same general area, but a few do have harmful counterparts—for example, the common dandelion, which is not only tasty but contains a considerable amount of vitamin A. From a written description, it could be confused with tansy ragwort, a noxious weed that has been shown to be harmful when eaten in even small quantities. Because of this similarity tansy ragwort has been included in the section on dandelion and in the section on poisonous plants. Fortunately, the ragwort soon grows quite tall, and after a few weeks in spring is no longer in danger of being confused with the dandelion.

Water hemlock looks much like several wild edibles you will find in this book, yet is probably the most poisonous plant on the continent. A few grams of water hemlock will kill a horse; even a few drops of the oil from its roots is enough to prove fatal to a man. Water hemlock is described in the chapter on poisonous plants. *It is essential that you be able to identify the water hemlock before you go foraging.* You could innocently touch it then transfer the toxin, an oily fluid, to a familiar edible and poison yourself.

None of the fungi or mushrooms, ranging from fine edibles to deadly poisons, have been included because they do not provide high levels of nutrition or energy, and they are hard to identify positively. Several excellent guidebooks are available and should be used whenever mushrooms are collected.

Every attempt has been made to provide a means for positive identification of the wild edibles discussed in this guide. Photographs taken under the best possible conditions appear with most descriptions. Drawings have been made of each plant. In a few cases, the drawn figure is sufficient to identify common or unique species, so no photographs were included. In most instances the photos just make sure you don't pick up something that will be harmful.

The Drawbacks: It is difficult to believe there are drawbacks to collecting wild edibles even though it often becomes arduous to gather enough for a meal. While blackberry picking can be backbreaking, the reward of a thick blackberry syrup over a winter morning's hotcakes is remembered long after the aches go away. The thought of ice cream topped with homemade jam spurs you on in the fall and keeps you picking even with scratched hands, sore knees,, and a sunburn. Although many of the plants are easy to collect, a few take time and effort.

Grinding a rough flour between two stones is also hard work, but after you eat your first batch of biscuits made from it, you won't complain again.

If there is a serious drawback in collecting wild edibles, it is that some have been rendered inedible by man. The wild plants have suffered from polluted water, defiled earth, and fouled air, so be careful where you collect them. Take aquatic plants only from waters that are not chemically polluted and don't collect leafy plants from areas of high industrial air pollution.

For the same reasons, don't collect wild edibles alongside the roadway. Exhaust fumes from passing cars are often absorbed by the plants, making their lead content far above levels safe for consumption. Usually, if you are far

Water hemlock

enough from the road that dust hasn't collected on the leaves, you are on safe ground. Along paved highways, stay at least 25 feet from the shoulder or ditch line.

In areas of heavy air pollution such as an industrial park, foliage may absorb fatal concentrations of lead and mercury from the air. Plants are often affected for a distance of several hundred yards from the source of the pollutant.

In areas of roadside spraying, which is becoming more commonplace along many secondary or country roads, you'll have to move beyond the swath that was treated with herbicides. Although they are not particularly strong poisons, they certainly aren't good for you. Some of the highly specialized sprays, such as 2-4-D or 2-4-5-T, are selective compounds that affect only broadleaf plants, but the chemical is still present on those plants that haven't been killed by it.

Foraging: A special activity related to collecting wild edibles is "foraging," an important part of pioneer life in America and a regular part of a family's activity across much of Europe.

Today, foraging may indicate the collection of wild plants for consumption at home *or* in the field, especially as part of hiking and camping activities. The camper with a mobile kitchen at his disposal just collects the wild edibles he likes or wants to try, turns on the stove, and turns out a delightful and different dinner.

If your foraging is part of a backpack trip, I'd suggest that you fix up a light "foraging kit" similar to mine. It's compact, easy to carry, and makes the eating great. Besides salt and pepper, you want a few small containers that won't spill in the pack. In one of the larger containers (a plastic prescription bottle is ideal), take some cold bacon drippings—a valuable addition if you fry some of the fleshy roots. Another container should hold a generous supply of butter for sauteing wild onions or leeks, spreading over wild-flour biscuits or hotcakes, or topping off a dish of steaming greens. A few ounces of a spicy oil-and-vinegar dressing makes the salads a lot better. A small flask of lemon juice makes many of the greens or salads sparkle with flavor. Three other items you'll enjoy are honey (a small squeeze bottle from the local supermarket), small container of baking powder (essential if you plan on using grains or pollens to bake rough-ground bread, biscuits, or cakes), and a couple of ounces of sugar for use with a few of the plants or berries.

The foraging kit is completed with three simple utensils: a knife other than your regular camping or hunting knife, a one-teaspoon measuring spoon, and a simple wire-screen sieve. The latter is indispensable for parching grains, cleaning nuts and berries, burning leaves for natural seasonings, and straining vegetables for thick, creamy soups. You might want to add an item or two that appeal to your own particular taste—seasoned salt, onion or garlic salt, and powdered chili pepper, for example.

I keep all these together in a handy small nylon stuff bag that can be tucked away in a corner of my pack, where it adds only about a pound to my load but hours of enjoyment to my outing. Your usual pots and pans are fine for cooking wild edibles. (A companion of mine years ago made up a special cook kit of three tin cans that fitted inside one another and had coat-hanger handles. He kept his foraging gear inside the smallest tin and a square foot of wire screen folded between the two outer cans. In one compact parcel he had utensils, spices, condiments, sugar and syrup, eating gear, and coffeepot—and the whole package didn't cost over a dollar.)

Choosing The Plant To Eat: There is one point that bears repeating: EAT ONLY THOSE PLANTS YOU KNOW ARE EDIBLE! Do not try unidentified plants.

Of the more than 14,000 plants that grow west of the Rockies, only about 2500 are actually known to be edible. Another 2000 or so are known to be harmful or poisonous. That leaves about 10,000 that we simply don't know about. That big majority had best remain unknown to us until they have been tested, and a camping trip or a back-country hike is not the place to do it. Over the years, a number of people have been poisoned in the field simply because they placed credibility in a couple of long-lasting myths. First, one old wives' tale would lead you to believe that you can eat any plant you see the animals eat. After all, they eat wild plants exclusively and they should know. Well, it just *ain't necessarily so!*

The squirrel, for example, can eat the deadly fly amanita mushroom with impunity, yet this mushroom is poisonous to a human being. The pig—whose digestive system is remarkably similar to ours—can eat large quantities of raw acorns. A human being who thus indulged would very likely endure great suffering and escape with no less than a badly damaged liver.

The second, more dangerous myth, concerns alleged "edibility tests" for wild foods. For many years, a variety of authors, even in survival manuals, have advocated a supposedly simple test for determining the safety of a plant.

According to these "experts," you begin by putting a small quantity of the food in your mouth and immediately spitting it out. If no burning or irritation occurs, you put another small quantity in your mouth, chew it, and again spit it out without swallowing. This step is repeated after waiting four hours or so. Then (provided you are still alive), you actually eat a small bite of the plant, wait twelve hours, and repeat the eating process. You must do this several times before you can assume the plant is safe.

Let's look at the facts that surround some of the known poisonous plants. Suppose the plant you choose for this experiment is water hemlock. At step one, you'd have put a powerful toxin in your mouth. Even if you spit it out instantly, the amount of deadly poison already mixed with your saliva would almost certainly kill you. Available information, generally obtained through an autopsy, indicates that only about 40 percent of all cases survived *any* oral contact with this plant! So you flunked the "edibility test" even before you got started.

Assuming the plant allowed you to get to the chewing stage, you might have one of the species that contain crystalline oxalic acid. At the slightest pressure from your tongue, the sharp crystals would penetrate the lips, gums, and tongue. If the plant were common *dieffenbachia,* by the time half an hour had passed, your lips and tongue might have swollen to the point where you could not breathe. You might need a tracheotomy (a luxury seldom available in the woods) to save your life. You failed again.

Even if the plant is edible, the entire testing process takes a minimum of 96 hours, during which you can't eat anything else for fear of affecting the reliability of the experiment. That means that under the most difficult of conditions, you would go four days without eating—hardly a practical approach to survival.

The fact is just this simple: eating any plant you aren't sure about can have drastic results. That includes the small amounts necessary for the so-called "edibility test."

Collecting and eating wild plants is a great recreational experience. Eat those plants that you know are safe, and foraging will provide you with fun, new tastes, and an expanded awareness of the outdoors. o

CHAPTER 2
Leaves, Stems, Bulbs, and Roots
and what to do with them

Just as you don't go into the market and order "a couple pounds of vegetables," you don't have to go into the woods and take the first thing that comes along. You can, in fact, be pretty choosy.

Some of the vegetables described in the following section are plain old meat-and-potato foods, while others are an exotic experience in eating. Experiment!

To me, each of these plants is something of a personality, to be reckoned with in as many different ways as there are individuals. While one is an open-armed, benevolent old friend, another is a miserly little creep that gives up its treasure from a tightly clutched fist.

As you gather wild edibles, you will follow a trail that nature dictates, and it isn't always the easiest. You will collect your bounty from the mucky bottom of a swamp and from the rich, dark soil of the forest. You will climb the rocky crags of the mountains and trudge across the hot and windy grasslands — but they are there.

With the drawings, descriptions, and photographs, you should be able to absolutely identify the plant you are seeking. If you can't, chances are you are looking at something else. In time, they will become as familiar to you as they are to me, and maybe you too will see the dainty little ballerina dancing in the quiet winds of the prairie grasses, or the bawdy Barbary madam of foul talk and fair heart, settling her bouncy bulk alongside a laughing stream. ○

ARROWHEAD *(Sagittaria latifolia)*
DUCK POTATO, WAPATO

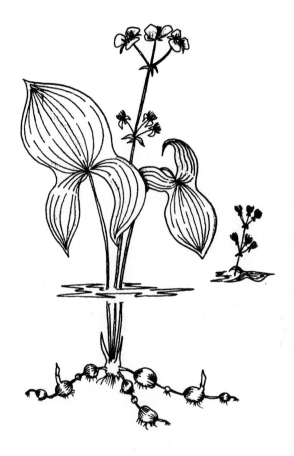

    A common but incredibly beautiful aquatic plant, the arrowhead is found throughout much of North America as well as Asia and eastern Europe. It is occasionally sold in modern grocery stores in predominantly Chinese districts of the United States.

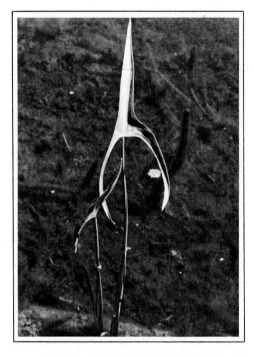

The young leaves show the unique shape. Note the water level is at about mid-stem in this incredibly clean pond.

Arrowhead was a valued part of the diet of the American Indian, finding wide usage across the country and into Canada. Western tribes called the plant "wapato," a name that was also used for the elk, another major contributor to the economy of everyday life in the villages. Both were available at virtually every season in an age when preservation of food was difficult. Arrowhead tubers could be collected from the mud that lined the bottom of the frozen winter ponds.

Our extensive records of the early uses of this plant reflect the importance it had to the Indians, explorers, and early settlers. Lewis and Clark purchased large quantities of arrowhead during their travels to the Northwest and subsisted mainly on them during the winter of 1805-1806. At that time, arrowhead and camas lily were the two major vegetables used by the Indians.

The tubers are the part to collect. The leaves and stems were not used by the Indians, and probably should not be tried. Although some people claim to have used the leaves, they contain a milky fluid that is bitter and unpalatable. There is no evidence that the leaves are poisonous, although they have not been readily used in the past.

These mature leaves rest on nearby limbs of shoreline bushes.

Habitat and distribution: Arrowhead grows in reasonably clear water in ponds and lakes and along slow-moving streams. It is generally confined to shallow water and is rarely found in more than two feet of water. While abundant in much of the country, it may be absent from large areas.

Description: Arrowhead is an aquatic perennial with a slim fleshy stem growing from a network of tubers under the soft underwater mud. Leaves have a definite arrowhead shape. They are parallel-veined, deep green, and may be emergent or floating on the water.

In the field: To collect the tubers, wade in the shallows and dislodge them with your feet or a stick. They float to the surface when so disturbed and are readily picked up. It is simpler to use a long-handled shovel or hoe to dislodge them from the muddy bottom of the swamp or pond. Pare the tubers and eat them raw or cooked. The raw plant tastes something like potato and has been

Young plants and dislodged tubers float in very shallow water. The tubers at this stage are quite soft.

described as superior to an Irish potato in the journals of Lewis and Clark. I tend to agree with that assessment. Boiling or roasting the tubers really brings out their flavor.

The baked, boiled, or roasted root is a treat in the field. I have pared, sliced, and fried the roots, but they tend to break up as they cook, which coincidentally makes them excellent for mashing and serving with gravy or butter. Wrap unpeeled tubers in foil or place them in the coals of your campfire for roasting, then serve with salted butter. Combined with a backpacker's dried meat and a green vegetable, they make a fitting end to a beautiful day along one of our lowland trails. (One of my most memorable meals in the woods came during a survey trip into the west Cascades of Washington. The party chief made a dinner of roast arrowhead, stinging nettle, and fresh cutthroat trout garnished with wood sorrel and mint. After several days of government-issue sausage and hard crackers, it was a banquet!)

In the kitchen: Consider arrowhead for its delicious taste and great flexibility in the camp or kitchen. It doesn't take long to gather a nice supply of arrowhead, and you may find yourself with several pounds in a bucket on the back porch. Fortunately, this versatile vegetable lends itself to dozens of recipes and endless experimenting in the comfort of your own kitchen. Here are a few of my favorites.

ARROWHEAD SAUTE

OLIVE OIL *or* BUTTER
3 tablespoons

SMALL ARROWHEAD TUBERS
24

SALT *and* PEPPER *to taste*
PAPRIKA *sprinkle*
CHIVES *or* PARSLEY

Heat the oil or butter in a heavy saucepan. Turn the peeled tubers in the oil until coated, then cover the pan and cook slowly until tender. Season to taste and sprinkle with paprika. Just before serving, sprinkle with finely chopped chives or parsley. Side dish for 4.

This is a simple and delicious way to try this fine vegetable. Another time, you may want to get fancier.

ARROWHEAD SWISS SCALLOP

ARROWHEAD TUBERS
4 cups peeled and sliced

BUTTER *2 tablespoons*

SALT *and* PEPPER *to taste*
SWISS CHEESE *1/2 cup grated*
PARSLEY

Peel the tubers and slice them in ¼-inch slices, boil, and let cool. Butter a small casserole dish generously. Over a layer of tubers, sprinkle salt, pepper, and grated cheese. Repeat until all the tubers are used. Bake for about 45 minutes or until the arrowhead is tender and the cheese melted all through. Garnish with a final sprinkling of cheese and chopped parsley. Serves 6.

This casserole scallop is really great with pork chops or a small baked salmon. Serves 6.

ARROWHEAD AND LEEK SOUP
(Mudfoot Vichyssoise)

MEDIUM WILD LEEK *3*
SMALL ONION *1*
BUTTER *2 tablespoons*
ARROWHEAD TUBERS *3 cups*
peeled and sliced

CHICKEN STOCK *3 cups*
CREAM *1 cup*
SALT *and* PEPPER
WATERCRESS *1/2 cup chopped*

Mince the leeks and onion and saute them in the butter. Simmer along with the arrowhead roots for 15 minutes in the chicken stock. Put them through a fine sieve or blender, return to the stock, and add the cup of cream. Season to taste and serve hot or cold, garnished with chopped watercress. Serves 6.

This is about the finest soup you'll ever eat. If you are in the bush, just chop the root, leek, and onion, simmer in broth, and forget the cream. It's a chicken chowder you won't forget. Incidentally, the "Mudfoot" name was added by a friend who went arrowroot gathering with me when I used the old Indian method of gathering and dislodging the tubers with my bare toes. In later years, both my feet and my curiosity have waned, and I prefer a stick or shovel!

BALSAMROOT *(Balsamorhiza* species)

There are nine species of balsamroot in the Northwest as well as a group of closely related sunflower varieties. To try to separate these here would be academic and a waste of time, since all are similar and are eaten in the same ways. Some types are more desirable than others, but only because they have larger roots and are thus easier to collect and prepare. The balsamroots are valuable as a wild edible because they have oily seeds — one of the few ready sources of vegetable oil to use in cooking, making a butter substitute, or formulating your own wild salad dressings.

Balsamroot is another plant that found wide acceptance among the North American Indians. The roots, seeds, young shoots, and leaves were all used in the cooking pot in a variety of ways. Even though the Indians prized the root above the other parts, the flowers were nonetheless collected in large quantities and the oil extracted from their seeds. The oil was a commodity that white explorers and settlers eagerly traded for and soon became a source of comparative wealth for many tribes. Early records indicate that some tribes, particularly in the Plains country, built substantial industries involved in producing balsam oil. (At the time, only the safflower and sunflower provided regular vegetable oils; corn oil extraction wasn't discovered for many more years.)

The seeds were also used for a fine white flour that was easily ground on the flat stones of the Indian village. It made a light, nutritious bread that was a staple, at least for part of the year, among many communities.

Habitat and distribution: The balsamroots generally prefer the drier, rocky ground away from the coastal region, but at least one variety flourishes in drier coastal areas. One or more is usually found everywhere except the very arid or desert regions.

Description: The several varieties of balsamroot and spring sunflowers have different types of leaves, but all share a showy golden flower. The combination disk-and-ray flowers, by far the best identifying feature, are somewhat coarse. The center disk may be yellow or brown, but the petals on the rays are always yellow or deep yellow. One or several blossoms may occur from a given cluster of flowers. The golden "sunflower" blossom is the key to identifying any of the varieties.

In the field: The cluster of flowers of balsamroot is easy to collect; just pluck it from the fleshy stem and put it into the collection bag. The roots are often large and take a certain amount of laborious digging because they are almost always found in rocky or gravelly soils. Eat the roots raw or cooked. The favorite method of the Indians was to wrap the roots in large wet leaves and bake them in the coals of a firepit. My own experience with these roots has

BALSAMROOT *(Balsamorhiza* species*)*

The several varieties of balsamroot share a showy golden flower.

shown that they are tough and rather bitter raw but excellent when cooked, especially if the root is candied or otherwise treated with a sweet preparation.

Eat the seeds roasted like sunflower seeds, without the bother of cracking away a tough outer shell. After a light roasting, they are easily ground into an excellent flour. (I prefer to grind flower seeds or pollen rather than wild grains, because they are easier to work with and produce a lot more flour for the same amount of work.)

To extract the valuable oil from the seeds, vigorously boil them in a large pot. The oil is easily skimmed off the top and collected in a separate container. It helps to bruise or lightly crush the seeds before boiling.

Peel and trim the large oily root before cooking.

In the kitchen: I prefer the seeds and flour over the greens or roots, but several fine dishes are made from the roots. I don't bring in the shoots and leaves for cooking. They aren't all that great, and much better greens are usually available at the same place during the same season.

BUTTER-BALSAM BUBBLE

BALSAMROOTS *1 pound* BROWN SUGAR *1/2 cup*
BUTTER *1/2 cup, melted* SMALL MARSHMALLOWS *1/2 cup*

Boil the freshly peeled balsamroots until they are tender. Place in a 2-quart baking dish. Pour the butter evenly over the roots. Sprinkle about half the brown sugar over the buttered roots, then spread the marshmallows in an even layer over all. Sprinkle the remainder of the sugar over the top and bake in a moderate oven until the sugar and marshmallows have melted into a thick, rich crust. Serve with a roasted fowl and dressing, or as a wonderful side dish to a pot roast of venison. Serves 6.

PINE AND BALSAM GORP

SUGAR *1/2 cup*
WATER *1-1/2 cups*
PINE NUTS *1 cup, raw*

BALSAM SEEDS *1 cup, roasted*
RAISINS *1/2 cup*
MILK *(optional)*

Dissolve the sugar in 1-1/2 cups of water to make a thin syrup. Soak the nuts, seeds, and raisins in the syrup for about an hour, stirring occasionally. Drain and remove the bulk (called gorp) and allow to dry in the sun for a day or two, until the whole is dried and lightly coated with sugar. Gorp is a high-energy food used by hikers and backpackers for trail snacks. It makes a fine breakfast with a little milk poured over it. Makes 3 cups for snacks.

GOLDEN BALSAM DRESSING

BALSAM OIL *4 tablespoons*
CIDER VINEGAR *3 tablespoons*
GARLIC SALT *1/2 teaspoon*
LEMON PEEL *1/2 teaspoon grated*

FRESHLY GROUND PEPPER *1/2 teaspoon*
PARSLEY *1/2 teaspoon chopped*

Mix all ingredients well by shaking vigorously in a closed bottle or stoppered cruet. Shake again just before pouring over a fresh salad. This dressing is tangy, but not overpowering. It is truly great over a salad of lamb's quarters, broad-leaved plantain, and avocado. Makes about ½ cup.

BALSAM BREAKFAST CAKES

BALSAM FLOUR *1-1/2 cups*
SALT *1 teaspoon*
SUGAR *3 tablespoons*
BAKING POWDER *1 teaspoon*

MILK *1 cup*
WHOLE EGG *1*
BLACKBERRY-MINT JELLY *or* MAPLE SYRUP

Mix dry ingredients thoroughly. Add the milk and egg to a well in the center of the dry mixture and beat briskly with a wooden spoon or whip until a few small lumps remain. Bake on a very hot lightly greased griddle until bubbles form. Turn and bake about a minute. Serve with blackberry-mint jelly or a rich maple syrup. Serve with scrambled eggs and a chopped venison breakfast steak for the finest breakfast you ever ate. Makes about 8 medium-size cakes.

Balsamroot seeds, oil, and roots are among the most valuable of all the wild edible plants that you can find. Many of us drive past vast fields of this fine plant, never realizing the treasure it stores. As you begin to use balsamroot, your eating fun will be limited only by your imagination!

BEARGRASS *(Xerophyllum tenax)*
BASKET GRASS, PINE LILY

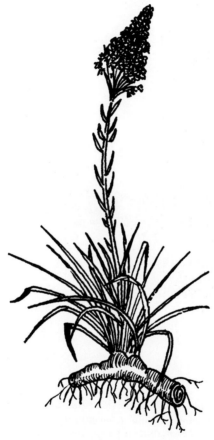

(color photo, page 170)

Almost anyone who ventures into the higher mountains in the early summer has seen this plant showing off beautiful stalks of white flowers. Even after the flowering season, the tall stalks remain upright and prominent. At other times of the year, the plant goes almost unnoticed, being confined to a tuft of evergreen grassy leaves.

Beargrass

Beargrass was not important to the early settlers, growing well above the places they usually chose for homesites and farms. The Indian, however, gathered it both as a food and a hardy weaving material from which baskets, ceremonial articles, and even clothing were made. The fibrous roots were used as a food and were popular in many cultures.

The leaves were often used in the early trade baskets that are presently in museums and other artifact displays. Combined with the bark of young cedars, intricate red and yellow patterns were developed that accurately identified the tribe from which the basket came. The cedar bark was rubbed to a glossy red polished finish that neatly complemented the roughened beargrass leaves.

Beargrass got its common name from an early supposition that bears dug up the plants and ate the roots. They probably do eat the roots, but not in the quantities that some people think. I once spent an hour watching a black bear rooting around on a high slope near Mount Adams in Washington, presumably digging out roots of beargrass, which were fairly common on the slope. After much laborious excavation, the bear came up with a large hoary marmot in its jaws. It immediately took off with its catch, heading for the timber far below. Subsequent investigation of the area showed that the beargrass roots scattered about were all intact. The digging had been solely to unearth the marmot from its underground burrow, and the roots had been incidental victims of that frenzied search.

I suspect that much of the bear's reputation for eating beargrass came from similar observations of their search for marmots, which are often found among the large stands of beargrass that provide a large percentage of their diet.

Habitat and distribution: Beargrass is invariably found at the middle elevations on mountainous slopes. It grows on steeply sloping ground and favors open areas rather than shaded or moist ones. It is particularly abundant in the shallow soils associated with talus slides and very rocky hills.

Description: Beargrass produces an erect flowering stalk from a mass of grasslike basal leaves. Small leaves extend up the thick stem. These small leaves are sharply pointed and needle-shaped, but the basal leaves resemble large clumps of grass. The flowers are white, and clustered in a large conical head. The large flowering stalk usually stands through the summer following the flower. These plants probably bloom only once every several years, so it is an advantage to learn to recognize them from the tufts of grass during nonflowering years.

In the field: Lift beargrass roots from the ground by pulling up at the base of the tuft of leaves. Sometimes, in better soil conditions, it is necessary to dig the roots up with a stick or shovel. Pare off the dark outer skin and very fibrous layer and use the more tender inner core as food. Even so, it is quite fibrous and tough and requires considerable cooking. It is best used in long-cooking dishes such as stews. Slow roasting or boiling is recommended. The roots are edible raw, but their very toughness makes that undesirable.

In the kitchen: This excellent root is quite fibrous and not particularly flavorful. Although it does require long cooking, it tends to absorb flavors from other foods, a trait that makes it particularly good in meaty stews and other combination dishes where its flavor is augmented. Try it in these and other dishes.

SHEEPHERDER'S STEW

BEARGRASS ROOTS *2-1/2 pounds*
MUTTON *1-1/2 pounds in
1-inch cubes*
ONIONS *1/2 cup sliced*

SALT *and* PEPPER
MUTTON STOCK *2-1/2 cups*
BAY LEAF *1*
PARSLEY

Slice the pared beargrass into very thin pieces. Put the beargrass, mutton, and onions into a heavy pot. Season and pour the stock over. Add the bay leaf and simmer the whole over low heat for 2-1/2 hours, or until the meat and root are tender. Sprinkle chopped parsley over the top and serve from the heavy pot. Serves 6 hungry campers.

With fresh biscuits and a salad, this is a fine meal. It was developed by Basque sheepmen, who served it with cordial hospitality and a completely unpronounceable name in the Idaho mountains.

BEARGRASS CHOWDER

BEARGRASS ROOTS *1 pound*
MILK *3 cups*
CLAMS *1/2 cup chopped*
ONION *1/2 cup chopped*

BACON *2 strips, chopped*
BUTTER
WHOLE KERNEL CORN *1/2 cup*
SALT *and* PEPPER

Boil the pared beargrass roots until very soft (30 minutes or more). Mash the roots to a rough consistency. Mix with the milk and bring to almost boiling. Meanwhile, lightly saute the clams, onions, and bacon in butter. Add this to the milk and beargrass and lower the heat. Add the corn, season to taste, and simmer for about 15 minutes. Serves 6.

BROWN BEARGRASS BULLY

BEARGRASS ROOTS *1-1/2 pounds*
SALT *and* PEPPER

BUTTER *2 tablespoons*
BEEF STOCK *1/2 cup*

Boil the whole, pared roots for about 20 minutes. Drain and set aside. Line a loaf pan with foil and put the roots in, allowing plenty of foil to completely seal the package. Season the roots, dot with butter, and pour the beef stock over the beargrass. Seal the foil tightly and bake in a moderate oven for 1-1/2 hours or until the roots are completely steamed in the stock. The beargrass will be moist and tender, flavored by the beef. Serve as a complement to a hearty beef pot roast. Serves 4.

BEDSTRAW *(Galium boreale)*

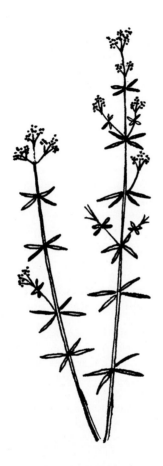

   Across the shaded woods you find a half dozen or so varieties of the common bedstraw, but the differences between any two are so minute that only a trained botanist can tell them apart.

The bedstraws were named because they were once used as fillers for mattresses or for rough beds. After drying, the plant tends to retain a little resiliency. It is awfully noisy to sleep on, but in the bush, it makes a comfortable mattress for your sleeping bag.

(In past years, many woodsmen have advocated the use of green boughs for a bed, but the boughs have some pretty hard limbs holding themselves together, and the damage caused by everyone in the woods chopping off a few limbs can be catastrophic. Although it is advisable to carry your own pad, no one objects to gathering bedstraw, which grows in profusion. The same cannot be said of many other materials, including fir or pine limbs.)

Habitat and distribution: Bedstraw is found growing under timber in virtually all areas of the western United States and Canada, and several forms exist throughout the continent, except for the treeless plains and deserts.

Description: Bedstraw is easily recognized by its square stems and regular whorls of four to eight leaves; the leaves are linear, lightly veined, and pale green. Before the seeds appear, tiny blossoms of white, pink, or pale green can be seen. The delicate stem usually climbs on other nearby plants. Generally it is too weak to stand alone, and if no support is nearby, the entire plant lies prostrate on the ground.

The plant is further recognized by a series of small curved hairs that grow along the stems and leaves. These recurved hairs are far too small to cause injury or even discomfort, but are efficient at hitching a ride on clothing or skin. The tiny seeds have harmless burs around them that need not be removed for use.

In the field: Bedstraw's greatest value, for our purposes, lies in the fact that it makes an excellent coffee substitute in the woods. You can gather the seeds, which grow in thick clusters at the top of the plant, by the handful and dry them. Then boil or percolate them into a fine coffee. There is almost no difference between the flavor of bedstraw seed and regular coffee.

In the kitchen: Other than coffee, I have had no experience with this plant, and I doubt that there are many other uses. You might experiment a little, but you will probably find this drink is its only practical—and delicious—use.

Note the small curved hairs on the stems and leaves.

BULRUSH *(Scirpus* species)
TULE

There are over 20 edible species of bulrush. *Scirpus validus* and *S. acutus* are the most valuable and tastiest. All have edible roots and produce large numbers of seeds on the stems.

Bulrush is another important food plant that you can use, in one way or another, throughout the year. It was a dietary staple for many Indian tribes, but never found much acceptance from the early settlers.

Although the root was often used as a starchy food, the Indians relished the sweet young shoots as a potherb and the seeds for a gruel and fine flour. The young shoots, which appear in the fall, were a welcome relief from the dry and mature foods of the previous three months.

In this species the seeds appear along the sides near the tops of the stalks.

BULRUSH *(Scirpus validus)*

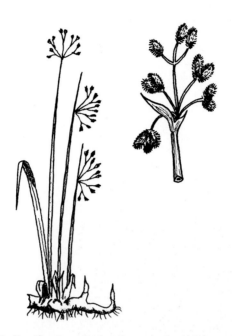

Habitat and distribution: Bulrushes are found in very damp ground, generally around swamps, ponds, and streams. They occur in virtually every area where there are large amounts of rich, wet soil. At least a few varieties can be found in all of North America.

Description: The various bulrushes are characterized by long, narrow, basal leaves that are quite tough and fibrous. In a few cases, the leaves are reduced to basal sheaths. Roots are heavy and tubular, covered with a fibrous brown skin and many root hairs. Stalks rise abruptly from the roots and may reach five or six feet in a few species, although two or three feet is more common. Pollen, flowers, and seeds may be borne on top of the stem or found showing along the side near the top. Stalks are hollow, pithy, and round or triangular in cross-section. Roots of several plants tend to intertwine, forming a solid platform in the marshy ground.

In the field: Young shoots found in the early fall among the old summer leaves are gathered and eaten raw or boiled. They add flavor and crispness to a salad or a stew.

You can dig the roots from the soft ground and scrape or peel them before cooking. Roast or boil them, or slice and fry them in a greased skillet. Boil the root until very soft and make into a gruel that can be eaten or dried into a white flour. The flour is excellent for making hotcakes by adding enough water to reach the desired consistency plus a bit of butter or fat. Mix in a few huckleberries for a fine breakfast.

Grind the seeds and pollen into a coarse flour that is good for baking-powder biscuits or any other general baking need.

You can boil young roots into a thin syrup that makes a substitute for sugar and is excellent over a combination of cracked grains and nuts as a cereal. Bruise the roots well before boiling to make the sweetest syrup, which can be further thickened and sweetened by continuing to boil the liquid after the root mass has been removed.

In the kitchen: Because of the slight sweetness of the bulrush root, it is used in a variety of novel recipes, with a unique and delightful result. It takes a little experimenting to get used to bulrush root or flour, but the new tastes are well worth the effort you make.

BULRUSH-RICE SOUP

BEEF SOUPBONE *2 pounds*	BULRUSH ROOTS *1 cup sliced*
BUTTER *1 tablespoon*	SMALL ONIONS *2*
BULRUSH FLOUR *2 tablespoons*	WILD RICE *1/2 cup*
WATER *6 cups*	SOY SAUCE *1 tablespoon*
BULRUSH SHOOTS *1/2 cup sliced*	SALT *and* PEPPER

Rub the meaty soup bone with butter and coat with bulrush flour. Put in water to boil. Immediately add the bulrush shoots, roots, and onions, cut into eighths. Cover and simmer for about an hour. Add the wild rice and soy, season to taste, and continue to simmer for another hour or until the rice is plump and tender. Add water if necessary. Serves 6.

BULRUSH SHOOTS AND CHEESE

BULRUSH SHOOTS *2 pounds*	SHARP CHEDDAR CHEESE
MILK *3 tablespoons*	*1/2 cup grated*
EGG YOLK *1*	

Trim the bulrush shoots all about the same length and tie into serving portions with white string. Place bottom down in a pan of boiling water so the tips will only be steamed and the heavier stalks boiled. Cover tightly. Heat the milk and egg yolk and melt the cheese into it, stirring constantly. To serve, snip the string from each bunch of shoots, arrange on a plate, and pour the cheese sauce over. Side dish for 6.

This dish is a perfect complement to lamb chops or sugar-cured baked ham.

BURDOCK *(Arctium minus)*

Burdock is a common weed appearing in one of two forms. *Arctium minus* is by far the most prevalent, but *A. lappa* also appears in many sections. The differences are of no consequence for our purposes, since both are edible and handled the same.

Burdock was never very popular among the Indians; it took more work than many other plants and is not particularly flavorful unless cooked in special ways. One exception among a few tribes was the use of the peeled stalk as a confection. The stalk was boiled in honey and pine sap to make an excellent candy that could be stored by wrapping in burdock leaves. Except for the inevitable invasion by ants and other insects, it kept quite well. In some instances it was used as a trade item between tribes.

Other societies have used the burdock for centuries, and it is today widely cultivated in some parts of Europe and Asia. Successful hybridization has taken place, producing a large-stemmed plant that resembles a green rhubarb. The stem is still preferred with sweeteners, and it was a popular favorite for pie fillings in many countries.

Habitat and distribution: One of the two species is found in moist soil virtually across the continent; it apparently is excluded only from the arid and desert regions. It adapts well to elevations from sea level to about 3000 feet.

Description: Burdock is a large biennial with characteristic burs forming during the reproductive season. The burs are armed with hooked hairs that

Note the small leaves unfurling at the center of the plant.

The inner stalk is almost transparent green.

cling tenaciously to clothing and animal fur, thus distributing them. The leaves are large, soft, and deeply veined. They grow from a husky root on thick, fleshy stems. The branched stalk can support many pink or purple flowers which eventually develop into the heavy burs. Burdock does not develop flowers or burs until the second year. During the first season, the plant is a low-lying rosette of heavy leaves, developing a second-year spire that supports the flowers and seeds.

In the field: The roots, leaf stalks, and young shoots are all edible, but thoroughly cook them before eating to remove any bitterness. The mature burdock can become almost unbearable.

The root is much better as an ingredient in soups or stews than eaten alone. Peel and wash it, then boil in two waters, the first containing soda if available. As an alternative, lightly pound the roots between boilings to tenderize.

Carefully peel the young stems and shoots before cooking, since much of the bitter flavor is contained in the fibrous skin. They should normally be boiled in two waters, again to remove the bitterness. They are best when a sweetener is added to the second water or served over the portions. The inner pith of fireweed is a good additive to the boiling water to impart a sweet flavor to the burdock stems and shoots.

Although burdock is not one of my personal favorites, it can be made quite pleasant if handled and cooked correctly. When included in a home recipe, it undergoes a change in character that vastly improves the flavor.

One note of caution: in isolated incidents burdock leaves have been found to absorb large quantities of lead and other heavy metals from the earth and the air; never eat them. The leaves can also absorb selenium from certain soils, but concentrations in the roots, shoots, and stems would not be high enough to cause any difficulty if eaten in normal amounts. The leaves alone are to be considered dangerous.

In the kitchen: Although a bit difficult in the field, burdock lends itself well to a wide variety of uses on the dinner table. It imparts a slightly tart taste to many recipes.

BOILED BURDOCK IRISH DINNER

BURDOCK ROOTS *2 pounds*	LARGE ONIONS *3*
BURDOCK STEMS *1 pound*	LARGE CARROTS *6*
BAKING SODA *1/4 cup*	BAY LEAF
WATER *2 quarts*	SALT *and* PEPPER
CORNED BEEF BRISKET *3-4 pounds*	PARSLEY
	MUSTARD *or* HORSERADISH

In a large stewpot, boil the burdock parts in the soda for 30 minutes. Drain, rinse burdock and pot well, and refill with 2 quarts of fresh water. Boil the brisket and burdock together for 2 hours. Skim off the foam and fat; add the quartered onions and pieces of carrots. Boiling all, add the bay leaf and season to taste. When brisket is tender, drain and serve as a boiled dinner, garnished with parsley and mustard or horseradish. 8 generous portions.

QUICK BOUILLA-BURDOCK SOUP

POTATOES *1-1/2 cups diced*	GREEN ONIONS *4*
BURDOCK STEMS *1-1/2 cups peeled*	CRAWFISH TAILS *12, boiled*
CREAM OF TOMATO SOUP	SALT *and* PEPPER
1 10-1/2-ounce can	BUTTER
MILK *1 cup*	

Boil the potatoes and burdock stems together for 45 minutes. Drain and set aside. In a large saucepan, bring soup and milk to a boil, then reduce heat. Add the stems, potatoes, onions, and crawfish tails. Season to taste and simmer for about 30 minutes. Serve with a pat of butter in the middle of each bowl for a hearty, flavorful soup. Serves 4 to 6.

CAMAS LILY *(Camassia quamash)*
BLUE CAMAS, COMMON CAMAS

(color photo, page 162)

The blue camas is a beautiful spring wildflower whose range extends from British Columbia to as far south as Nevada, although the few varieties in Nevada and California may be rare.

Because it is readily identified for only a short blossoming period each year, the camas lily is not a staple among the wild edibles. The plant is available in substantial quantities in many areas, but without the flower it can be confused with the deadly white camas, quite accurately called the "death camas." The plants are almost identical in structure, but differ in both flower color and edibility. The two plants commonly are found growing in close proximity, but collect only the blue camas for food.

Blue camas has long been a staple of many Indian tribes and is still collected by a few small groups in semi-isolated places of the western states. The bulbs were often dug, transplanted to some place where they would remain until after the flowers had withered and gone. In this respect, it may have been the very first cultivated plant in some native societies.

The camas was not widely used by early white settlers. In some places, it was considered to be occasionally poisonous, owing probably to a mistake in collecting the plant and allowing a white camas bulb to get mixed in with the others. Some tribes had a special ceremony to mark the beginning of the blooming season of this flower, since that event heralded a favorite and long-awaited addition to the menu.

The nutritional value of the blue camas was analyzed in a recent research project on early Indian foods by the Oregon State University. There is a full listing of the nutritional values given in the table. It has a particularly high energy rating, which probably explains why it was accepted as such an important part of the diet of the Indian and the early settler.

Habitat and distribution: The blue camas is usually found in dry, rocky ground except for the alpine elevations and pure desert areas. It flourishes in semiarid plains but is found on suitable ground near ocean beaches and in other typically damp climates. It tends to grow only in locally abundant patches west of the Cascade Mountains, but is generally widespread elsewhere.

However, it is gradually losing some of its range to large-scale agricultural development and suburban growth. In a few places, it has been all but eliminated from earlier habitats. Where the plant is becoming scarce, don't collect in large numbers, if at all. Fortunately, it chooses ground that is often less desirable and thus seems protected from extinction.

Description: Blue camas is an upright perennial growing from an enlarged bulb. Without exception, the flower is pale blue, and several may occur on a single stem. The leaves are grasslike, tall, and erect. Oily seed pods

Blue camas

form as the flowers are disappearing. The pods are three- and four-sided, with quite definite corner ridges. NOTE: In a very few instances the flower of the blue camas fades to a white blossom. It can be distinguished from the cream color of the death camas but never collect it because of the chance of gathering a potentially deadly plant. Dig up *only* those bulbs that produce a flowering stalk with blue flowers.

Small blue camas bulbs

In the field: Only the bulb of the blue camas is known to be edible. The leaves and stems may gather lead or mercury from the air, particularly when found growing along roadways or near heavily industrialized areas, so don't experiment with them as an edible. Be content with the fine flavor and ease of collection of the bulbs, which are usually pulled directly from the ground. It is sometimes necessary to dig the shallow roots from the soil. Prepare the bulb, which tastes something like a new potato, by simply lifting the outer brown skin away, much as you do with an onion, which it closely resembles in appearance. You can eat it raw, but you'll probably prefer it roasted, steamed, boiled, or fried since the raw bulb is sometimes oily and rather glutinous. Camas bulbs tend to get soft and dark if overcooked. A shorter cooking time preserves both its flavor and attractive appearance.

In the kitchen: If you are fortunate enough to live or hunt where this plant is plentiful, it is a fine vegetable to carry home. Almost any recipe for new potatoes can be adapted to the camas, and you'll probably think of a lot of ways to use it.

CAMAS COCKTAIL

CAMAS BULBS *8, cut in quarters*
CRAWFISH TAILS *1/2 cup, boiled and peeled*
CATTAIL SHOOTS *1/4 cup chopped*
TOMATO SAUCE *1/2 cup*
CIDER VINEGAR *1 teaspoon*
ONION *1 tablespoon chopped*
CHILI POWDER *dash*
LETTUCE *or* DANDELION GREENS
LEMON WEDGES

Mix first 7 ingredients in a small mixing bowl. Spoon into individual cocktail glasses over a bed of fresh lettuce or dandelion greens. Garnish with lemon wedges. Serves 6 to 8.

This sharp, tangy appetizer will start any meal with conversation and flair!

CAMAS RAINBOW CREAM

WHITE SAUCE *2 cups*
CAMAS BULBS *1-1/2 cups*
GARDEN PEAS *1 cup*
FRESH CLOVER BLOSSOMS *12*

Prepare your favorite white sauce and simmer the camas bulbs and peas in it for about 15 minutes or until the bulbs are semitransparent. Add the fresh clover blossoms and simmer just 5 minutes to tenderize the clover. (The clover is far better if soaked in salted water for about 1/2 hour prior to use.) Serves 6.

This colorful dish is a fine complement to a halibut roast or stuffed fowl.

CAMAS SCALLOP SUPREME

CAMAS BULBS *3 cups sliced thin*
BUTTER *3 tablespoons*
FLOUR *1 tablespoon*
CATTAIL SHOOTS *1/2 cup chopped*
SMALL TROUT *6*
SALT *and* PEPPER
DRY MUSTARD *(optional)*
MILK *1-1/2 cups*
PAPRIKA *1 teaspoon*
PARSLEY
LEMON

Dot the camas with butter and flour; alternate in layers in a casserole with a thinner layer of chopped cattail and trout, seasoned with salt, pepper, and dry mustard (optional). Pour the milk over the dish and bake covered for 1/2 hour. Uncover, sprinkle with paprika, and bake for about 1 hour longer. Garnish with parsley and lemon. Serves 6.

Serve with boiled nettle or other leafy green vegetable. It's a simple dish that provides an outstanding use for wild edibles.

WILD CARROT *(Daucus pusillus)*
RATTLESNAKE WEED

The wild carrot is a familiar plant along the roadsides and in unused open ground. It is a common edible that is essentially the same as a domestic carrot, but with one very serious disadvantage: it closely resembles a couple of very dangerous plants—the water hemlock and Queen Anne's lace! The confusion among these plants extends even into the community of the popular botanist. It is for this reason that the lowly carrot has long been viewed with understandable suspicion. However, once you can accurately identify it you'll add a nutritious, valuable plant to your year-round larder of wild edibles.

The following description of this plant is perhaps more lengthy because you simply cannot afford to mistake it for any of the look-alikes that grow in

The foliage of wild carrot bears a strong resemblance to the domestic variety.

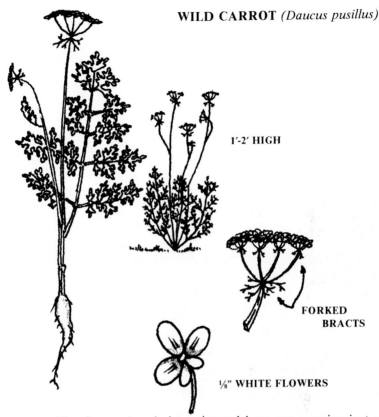

WILD CARROT *(Daucus pusillus)*

1'-2' HIGH

FORKED
BRACTS

⅛" WHITE FLOWERS

the same areas. The Queen Anne's lace pictured here was growing just a hundred yards from the wild carrots also pictured. My 13-year-old son consumed the carrot with a growing boy's gusto and no ill effects—but I can't be sure the same would have been true had he eaten the lace!

The edibility of Queen Anne's lace has long been in dispute, and it is not included in this book for that reason. I know people who eat the roots with no apparent problem, but I also know of verified cases of poisoning from the same plant. Whether this is attributed to a difference in growing conditions or an individual reaction to the plant I don't know, but it obviously is not recommended for general use.

In many places, particularly the drier regions, the carrot grows in profusion and was an important addition to the native diet. Early settlers used the plant in the spring and summer to brighten their dreary menu. In many

WILD CARROT *(Daucus pusillus)* *Edible*

PALMATE

CARROT

QUEEN ANNE'S LACE *(Daucus carota)* *Poisonous*

PINNATE

QUEEN ANNE'S LACE

places, it grows without intrusion of the Queen Anne's lace, so it can be collected in those places.

Nutritionally, as you can see in the table, it is quite similar to the cultivated carrot, with one notable exception; the lack of vitamin A. In the domestic variety, the majority of this vitamin lies in the carotine, which also gives it the bright orange color. The white root of the wild stock obviously doesn't have the pigment—nor the A vitamins!

Habitat and distribution: Wild carrot is found in dry, open areas and in places that had grass fires the previous season. Don't gather it along roadways, as the foliage can absorb lead from exhausts or lead could be on the leaves.

Description: In identifying wild carrot, it is imperative that you be able to identify water hemlock and poison hemlock on sight. Although the differences are obvious, there is a superficial likeness when the hemlocks are small. The greatest difficulty for most of us is differentiating between the carrot and Queen Anne's lace *(Daucus carota)*. Therefore, the two plants are compared throughout this description.

The wild carrot is a somewhat dainty, fernlike plant that has several upright branched stems. The leaves are palmately compound, consisting of many small ruffled leaflets. The leaves of Queen Anne's lace are *pinnately* compound (see accompanying sketches of the features of the leaves and roots). The carrot stems are heavily ribbed and covered with fine, thick hairs.

The flowers grow in compound umbels that look like umbrellas atop single stalks well above the leaf mass. Even though the umbels may be three inches across, the white or sometimes purplish flowers are very tiny.

The root structure of the carrot is essentially vertical, closely resembling a white domestic carrot. It is covered with a tough brown skin, and the inner core is surrounded by a layer of fibrous material. Queen Anne's lace has a thin, horizontal root that isn't at all similar to the carrot. Since only the root is edible, this characteristic is a good distinguishing feature. Moreover, the carrot root *smells* like a carrot, although that identification may not always hold true.

When viewed side-by-side the differences between carrot (left) and Queen Anne's lace are obvious.

The fibrous brown outer layer is pared away, revealing the snow white inner root. Young carrot roots tend to be bitter, but larger older plants, such as this one, are quite good.

In the field: Uproot the carrot, peel the root, and then cook it or eat it raw. Cooking is much better, since the outer layer of the root is fibrous and the inner core is almost as tough as the limbs of a tree! *Never* eat the greens!

In the kitchen: Use wild carrot in any cooked dish that calls for a common carrot. It especially lends itself to recipes that use brown sugar, honey, or maple syrup. The subtle differences between this and the domestic carrot are best brought out by a candied treatment.

KEVIN'S COOKED CARROT

ONION *1/2 cup chopped*   SUGAR *1 teaspoon*
BUTTER *3 tablespoons*   ZUCCHINI *1 cup diced*
WILD CARROT *2 cups shredded*   WATER *1/2 cup*
SALT *1/4 teaspoon*   PARSLEY

Saute the onion in butter for a few minutes, then add the carrots for just 2 minutes. Place these in a lightly greased baking dish. Sprinkle the salt and sugar over and stir in the uncooked zucchini. Pour 1/2 cup of water over, cover, and bake until the carrots are tender. The carrot will maintain a creamy whiteness while the onion and zucchini become somewhat transparent. Garnish with chopped parsley. Serves 8.

There are so many fine carrot recipes available that I won't include any further instructions, but will rely on your imagination. Get to know the delicate, delicious flavor of this wild edible.

CATTAIL *(Typha latifolia)*

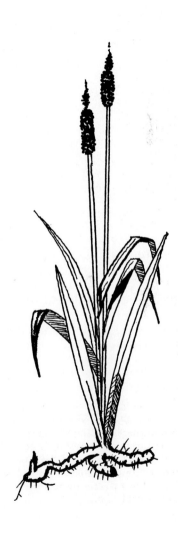

The easily recognized cattail is probably the most common and best known aquatic plant in the western hemisphere. It provides an easily collected food at any season. Even in winter, roots are dug from beneath the ice of a pond or marsh. Throughout the remainder of the year a few shoots appear, which are delicious even when they are large and older. The leaves are tough and not very tasty, and the peduncle (the round, central stalk that holds the spike) is too tough and tasteless to be of much value to the menu. During late summer and fall, however, the dark brown fibrous "cattail" contains a surprising amount of pollen, which is easily used for making rustic flour. (See Chapter 4 for instructions on making stone-ground flour from grains and pollens.)

The cattail root is an excellent foodstuff that is immensely valuable as a survival food. Handle the core, which is almost pure starch, like a potato. It provides a high-starch and relatively low-fat food that helps keep you full and maintains body heat.

Description: Cattail is characterized by tall slender stems topped with a dark brown spike. The flower arrangement is short-lived, but the spike usually remains until the following season. Each plant consists of a heavy underwater rootstalk, a half-dozen or more dark green narrow leaves up to three feet high, and two or more tall spires topped with flaring "cat's tails" from which the plant gets its common name.

In the field: After digging the rootstalk, peel it and remove the fibrous outer covering. Try the firm, white core sliced, diced, or boiled whole. Add a little salt and milk (or water) and mash. Serve with gravy or butter as you do mashed potato. Sliced roots fried and lightly salted are quite similar to country-fried potatoes. Wrap the pared roots in foil and roast them in the coals of a fire; they are delicious topped with butter, gravy, or sour cream.

Dry the rootstalk and pound it into a white flour that makes light breads and biscuits rivaling the best that can be made with "factory ground" wheat flours. Boil leftover mashed cattail root into a thick gruel and serve with sugar or wild honey at breakfast—a wilderness treat that can't be matched.

Raw young shoots have a distinctive taste of cucumber and are a favorite of most people who regularly include wild edibles in their diet. To gather young shoots, just grasp the younger leaves and pull straight up. Either the shoot comes away clean or a few root hairs remain. Trim the bottom of the shoot with a knife, peel away the outer two leaves, and it is ready to eat. The shoots are a great addition to soups and stews or boiled as a cooked vegetable. One of my favorite uses for the cattail shoot is in a salad. Combined with plantain and dandelion leaves and a few chopped mint leaves and stems, then topped with spicy oil-and-vinegar dressing, it is fit to set on the table at the finest black-tie sit-down dinner anywhere.

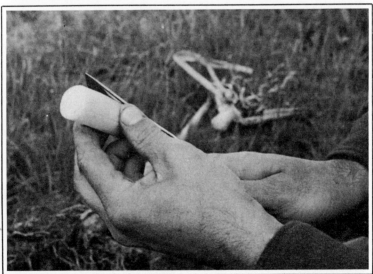

To prepare cattail shoots, cut away the root fibers. Then peel the stem.

To collect pollen, hold the brown spike over a container of some kind and strike it sharply with a stick. The pollen falls directly into your bucket or sack. Eat it raw, boiled into a thick mush, or ground into a rough, flavorful flour meal. Some people see the raw pollen as flavorful, but to me it has always had a musty taste, and I don't care for it in that form. Lightly ground, mixed with water, and baked into thin hotcakes, it is a different matter. With a little honey or syrup, they have a unique, delicious buckwheat flavor.

In the kitchen: The cattail is a fine plant that I enjoy eating as much as anything available in the grocery store, and the recipes are virtually endless. Clean your bounty as much as possible at the marsh so you don't bring home the small snails and bugs that live among them, and wash them well in fresh water since most of our swamps and ponds are somewhat polluted these days.

This is the plant that I generally use to introduce a novice to the joys of wild edibles, simply because the flavors of all parts are not unfamiliar, and people don't experience the trepidation that often accompanies a first attempt at something like stinging nettle, devil's club, or skunk cabbage.

A large cattail root may weigh as much as four pounds.

CATTAIL WILDERNESS STEW

VENISON or BEEF STEW *2 pounds*
CATTAIL ROOTS *2 pounds,*
cleaned and pared
SMALL ONIONS *6*
(wild if possible)

LARGE CARROTS *2, sliced round*
MEDIUM CATTAIL SHOOTS
6 sliced into 1-inch rounds
SALT and PEPPER
WILD MINT SPRIG *1*

Cut the venison or beef into small pieces. Slice cattail roots into 1/2-inch cubes. In a 3-quart saucepan or stewpot, put a single layer of meat, then a layer of cattail root, and a third layer of onion, carrot, and cattail shoots. Repeat the layering process until all the ingredients are used. Cover with water and cook slowly over low heat. Add salt and pepper to taste. After 1 hour, add the mint. Don't stir until almost done, normally about 2 hours. Serve piping hot with biscuits or bread. It is a thick, meaty stew that is equally at home in the hunting camp or dining room. Serves 8 to 10.

CHARLIE'S CATTAIL CHOWDER

MILK *3 cups*
CATTAIL ROOTS *2 cups*
cut in 1/4-inch cubes
MEDIUM ONION *1, chopped*
CLAMS or MUSSELS
1 cup finely chopped

BACON SLICES *2, crisp*
and finely crumbled or chopped
BUTTER *2 tablespoons*
SALT and PEPPER

Put the milk, cattail roots, and onion in a saucepan, bring to a quick boil, then simmer while you saute clams and bacon in a heavy skillet with the butter. When they are done, add them to the saucepan, butter and all. Season to taste. Simmer for 1/2 hour and serve with crackers or pilot bread. Serves 6.

This simple chowder—a West Coast favorite for years—is best made with razor clams, but any kind of good white clam will do. You may substitute a 6-1/2-ounce can of chopped clams from the store.

CATTAIL DELIGHT

WHITE SAUCE *1 cup*
FRESH CATTAIL SHOOTS *1/2 pound*

BLUE CAMAS LILY BULBS *12*

Make a thick white sauce according to your favorite recipe. Add the cattail shoots, trimmed to about 2 inches and sliced lengthwise, and the camas bulbs, cut in half. Simmer until the bulbs are soft and semitransparent. Serve as a side dish to roast meat or fowl—a gourmet's treat!

CHICKWEED *(Stellaria media)*

Common chickweed is one of the many varieties of wild edibles introduced from Europe, where it was widely cultivated as a table green. Following the advent of international trade in grains, chickweed was accidentally introduced to other countries and now thrives on every continent that has suitable climates. Because of the many common names for this plant, much confusion exists in its true identification. Most experts agree that the correct edible is *Stellaria media,* although others list a relative, *Alsine media,* as the common chickweed. The argument is largely academic since both are similar in flavor and appearance. Of the two, *S. media* is by far the more common.

The species has been used in Europe for centuries but never received widespread use by American Indians—even though more than one popular writer has described its use as a native potherb. The plant was actually introduced late in the eighteenth century and did not gain sufficient foothold to be accepted by the native communities in any quantity. It is somewhat romantic to have part of your dinner likened to an old Indian stew, but it probably wasn't so. If romanticism makes your wild dinner taste better, think of it as being on the menu of a fifteenth-century gypsy band in Bavaria!

Habitat and distribution: Chickweed is found in ground ranging from wet to quite dry, in open sun or shade, and especially along roadways and in the margins of cultivated fields throughout the continent. The extremities of chickweed's range seem to be subarctic Canada and the deserts of northern Mexico.

Description: Stems are quite weak, sometimes reclining, with many branches arising from the base. Stems are covered with fine hairs. Leaves are opposite; long petioled below, sessile on the upper part of the plant. The leaves are oval and rather sharply pointed. Small white flowers are borne in clusters at the top of each stem. Only the flower differs in the two major varieties of chickweed.

Although the plant is an annual, it frequently lives through the winter, especially in the southern part of the country, or during an unusually mild winter in the North. The leaves are still edible but require more cooking than in spring and early summer. The leaves and stems tend to become quite stringy and tough as the season progresses.

In the field: Only the youngest leaves are suitable for eating raw. Pluck the plant, stem and leaf together, and chop as a green in the springtime, or for a potherb or green vegetable the remainder of the year. In midsummer remove the blossoms before cooking. They are probably edible but do not have the pleasant taste of the rest of the plant. If you pull the roots with the plant,

CHICKWEED *(Stellaria media)*

discard them. They are undoubtedly safe to eat but are very tough and stringy—a condition that cooking doesn't greatly improve.

Since the rather fibrous leaves and stems don't "cook down" substantially from their raw volume, they are excellent to include in stews or other combinations. They can easily replace spinach, asparagus, or chard in any of your favorite recipes.

In the kitchen: Because of the rich, full flavor of chickweed, it is a favorite side dish for a dinner of meat or fowl. Many cooks prefer to use it plain or with the simplest condiments to preserve the flavor.

Chickweed

GYPSY CHICKWEED

CHICKWEED LEAVES *1 pound*

BUTTER *1 tablespoon*

OLIVE OIL *2 tablespoons*

GARLIC CLOVE *minced*

SALT

Rinse the chickweed in clear water, shake lightly, and place in a heavy skillet still wet. This is all the water you'll need in preparing this dish. Add the butter, olive oil, and garlic. Cook over high heat, covered, until a few wisps of steam rise from the edge of the skillet. Reduce the heat, add salt if necessary, and simmer until tender—about 5 minutes. Please don't overcook. Serves 4.

SICILIAN SILVERGREEN

SMALL ONION *1, chopped*

MUSHROOMS *1/4 cup sliced*

BUTTER *1 tablespoon*

OLIVE OIL *1 tablespoon*

CHICKWEED LEAVES *and* STEMS *1 pound*

CANNED ANCHOVIES *4*

PIMENTO *1 teaspoon chopped*

GARLIC SALT *1/4 teaspoon*

WATER *1/4 cup*

Saute the onion and mushrooms in the butter and oil. Add the chickweed and anchovies, roughly chopped into 1/2-inch pieces. Stir in the pimento and garlic salt. Add 1/4 cup of water and cook over high heat until the water evaporates, turning often. Reduce heat and simmer until the chickweed is tender and colorful. Serves 4.

This was a historic favorite of Sicilian fishermen for a light main course in hot summer weather.

CHICKWEED PARMESAN

CHICKWEED LEAVES *3 cups*

BUTTER *1 tablespoon*

MILK *2 tablespoons*

PARMESAN CHEESE *1/4 cup grated*

Boil the chickweed in a saucepan. As soon as the water reaches a high boil, reduce heat, cover, and simmer. Meanwhile, in a small saucepan, melt the butter in the milk. Don't let this boil. Add the Parmesan cheese, stirring constantly until it makes a thick sauce. Add cheese or milk to reach the required consistency. Serve on individual dishes with the sauce poured in a wide stripe over the chickweed—it adds a zesty tang, yet keeps the plant's delicate flavor. This common weed could never be better honored! Serves 6.

CLOVER *(Trifolium* species)

Almost everyone who has ever been off the pavement can recognize the kinds of clover that grow abundantly throughout North America. Of the dozens of clovers, probably red and yellow are the most abundant. The common white clover, a variant of yellow clover, is also edible. This plant is widely cultivated as pasture or forage for cattle, and many game departments have begun planting clover in remote clearings as winter feed for the browsing animals such as deer and elk.

The flowering plant is especially valuable as a survival food when cooked, since it is high in protein and is virtually impossible to mistake for any other. Even the tiniest of yellow varieties are edible, although they take a long time to collect. The common red and yellow plants are quite large, however, and are quickly picked and prepared.

When the flowers were ripe, many Indian tribes collected large amounts to dry for tea or to eat whole. They contain a sweet nectar—which attracts zillions of bumblebees to the clover-patch—and are a refreshing treat along the trail. The Indians also dried and ate the roots, after cooking, and they dried quantities of the leaves for smoking purposes. I have eaten clover

The clover leaves are marked by a pale green chevron effect.

CLOVER *(Trifolium repens)*

blossoms, leaves, and roots, but I frankly haven't had the urge to stuff a handful in my pipe. Maybe I'm missing something.

I discovered that at least some research has been done on the nutritive values of clover, but after laboriously copying the figures, I found that this research was done on behalf of the dairy industry. Doubting that my readers would be Holsteins, I forgot the whole thing!

Habitat and distribution: The several species grow in soils that range from rich to poor and wet to dry, and at all elevations up to subalpine. A few tiny varieties are found up to snow lines in early summer in the Rocky, Cascade, and Olympic mountain ranges.

Description: Only two species are discussed here *(Trifolium pratense* and *T. agrarium),* but all can be recognized from this description. The clovers are herbaceous annuals with compound palmate leaves divided into three leaflets. Rarely four leaflets will comprise the compound leaf and were once believed to have supernatural protective powers, thus the "lucky" four-leaf clover. The leaflets vary from round to very oblong and pointed.

The distinctive clusters of flowers are ball-shaped. The clusters range from less than one-fourth-inch in diameter to about an inch, depending on the species. The petals (corollas) may be white, yellow, pink, rose, red, or purple. The plants range from a few inches to over two feet in height. Stems and undersides of leaves are often slightly hairy.

In the field: The clovers are all edible raw, especially the flowers, but eat them in limited quantities since they are hard to digest. Clover leaves are fibrous so boil them fresh for as much as 10 minutes in quite salty water to bring out the best flavor, then serve with butter and lemon—delicious! The flavor isn't destroyed by prolonged cooking, as in the case with stinging nettles and many other wild greens. Even so, clover leaves and blossoms are a bit chewy. They have something of a spinach taste but are decidedly sweeter. Small wonder cows break down the fences to get into the clover field!

Pluck the leaves and blossoms from the thick stems and cook in boiling water until they are green and tender. The leaves turn a bright emerald-green after cooking—your tongue will remain tinted a faint green for an hour or more after dinner!

If the roots are collected, you can easily pull them from the soil. Snip off the lower tip to exclude the small mat of root hairs. The long, thin root is covered with a thin brown skin that can be rubbed off, exposing the white inner root. It is made of tough fibers so boil for a quarter-hour or longer to make them edible (or at least chewable!). The root has a sweet flavor, however, and is a fine addition to a soup or stew that simmers for a long while over the campfire.

If the roots and leaves are to be eaten raw, soak them in salt water overnight. They become quite digestable while retaining their sweet taste.

In the kitchen: Although the clovers are somewhat limited to being used as a fresh green vegetable, the blossoms lend themselves to a variety of colorful applications. (See the recipe for Camas Rainbow Supreme under camas lily, for example.)

CLOVER-BRIGHT SALAD

DANDELION GREENS 2 cups
MINT LEAVES 12
ONION 1, chopped
CLOVER BLOSSOMS 1 cup
MEDIUM CUCUMBER 1, sliced

SALMONBERRIES or
RASPBERRIES 1/2 cup
OIL-*and*-VINEGAR DRESSING
or LEMON

Tear the dandelion leaves into salad-size pieces. Mix with mint leaves, onion, and clover blossoms that have been soaked overnight in salted water. Place in a salad bowl and arrange the berries and cucumber slices over the top. Put the top sprig of the mint in the center for effect. Serve with a spicy oil-and-vinegar or other light dressing, or squeeze a fresh lemon over your salad and garnish with the peel. It is refreshing and colorful. Serves 4.

C AND C

CLOVER LEAVES 2 cups
BUTTER 1 tablespoon

MILK 2 tablespoons
CHEDDAR CHEESE 1/2 cup grated

Boil the clover leaves for about 10 minutes in fresh water. Meanwhile, melt the butter in the milk over low heat. Add the cheese and stir constantly until it melts into a very thin sauce. Add more milk if necessary. To serve, put half a serving into a small dish, pour the cheese over, and add the remainder of the individual portion on top. The cheese will become quite thick, almost hard, before you finish. This complements the texture of the clover and makes a bright, cheerful side dish for a dinner of fresh trout. Serves 4.

COLTSFOOT *(Petasites speciosa)*

Coltsfoot, also called butterbur, is a spectacular plant. The purplish-white flower occurs before the leaves are formed, so many people aren't able to recognize it after the flower withers, usually early in the spring. It was historically used by Indians in the Northwest and on the Canadian west coast as a substitute for salt, much in the same manner as the leaves from a cow parsnip.

Very little is known about the qualities of this stocky plant, and I have never experimented with it as a food. The shoots and leaves, although probably safe to eat, have not been satisfactorily tested. My only direct knowledge is in the use of coltsfoot as a seasoning, which I will pass along.

Note the characteristic leaves and stalk.

COLTSFOOT *(Petasites speciosa)*

Habitat and distribution: Coltsfoot requires rich, damp ground to support its heavy bulk and is generally found in areas of substantial rainfall. It is abundant on the Pacific coastal plain but decreases in frequency from north to south. It can be freely picked from this coastal shelf but don't take it from any appearance on the east Cascades or the Rockies, where it is rare.

Description: Coltsfoot is a thick-stemmed plant that bears flowers and seed at the top well before the leaves appear. The stout stalk appears to be covered with the remnants of old leaves, but they are a series of clasping bracts that are rounded and narrow with parallel veins. The flowers are purplish-white and clustered in a nearly semicircular head. The flowers have a sweet, heavy scent that is quite pleasant and extends through the woods far from the plant. The flower head turns to seed without any perceptible change in shape or color, which is an additional key to identification.

The leaves appear later, growing with almost upright petiole from the lowest bracts along the stalk. Occasionally leaves appear at higher bracts in older plants. They are deeply lobed into seven to nine divisions, each of which may be deeply toothed again. These leaves are about 12 inches across and have a woolly white hair on their underside.

In the field: Make the leaves into a pleasant salty seasoning by burning the dried leaves, then powdering the resultant ashes. Burn them over an open fire employing a wire basket to save the ashes. The native method was to roll the green leaves and dry them thoroughly. They were then set afire on a flat stone and the ashes collected.

The leaves and shoots are reputed to be edible after boiling, but there is no historic or scientific evidence to support this contention. Neither the texture nor the odor of the leaves would tempt me to try them.

Moreover, I have observed coltsfoot many times in the field, particularly along Washington's upper Cowlitz River, and have never seen any evidence that it was used as forage by deer and elk. I'm afraid I would approach this plant as an edible with caution.

In the kitchen: It's a fine, white substitute for salt—and as far as I know, that's it!

COW PARSNIP *(Heracleum lanatum)*

    Cow parsnip is, as might be expected from the Latin name's reference to Hercules, a giant of a plant. The cooked root is reminiscent of rutabaga, which it is related to, as a member of the carrot family.

    Cow parsnip was frequently used by western Indians to cure stomach cramps, gas, and other gastric disorders. The roots were cooked into a mushy pulp and fed to the afflicted member of the tribe, who soon got over the upset. The plant is also reputed to be effective in the treatment of epilepsy, but modern medicine has understandably withheld full endorsement of cow parsnip as a prescription item.

Since the cow parsnip is a member of the carrot family, it is also related to the water hemlock, so positive identification is essential before it is collected and cooked. The roots have the same aroma as the water hemlock, but it would be difficult to confuse with the much smaller hemlock plant. Nonetheless, caution is urged in collecting smaller cow parsnips so that a dangerous error won't be made.

Habitat and distribution: Cow parsnip is found in moist, rich soil, quite often near a source of water such as a stream or swamp. It is abundant along roadsides in the coastal plain west of the Cascades in Washington, Oregon, and northern California and occurs in substantial numbers in most other mountainous areas.

Description; The first clue to the cow parsnip's identity is the plant's size. It often reaches ten feet, although a plant about five or six feet is more common. The root is large, but not as big as you might expect from such a mammoth plant. The stems are hollow and have an aromatic, acidy smell. The huge compound leaves remotely resemble a maple. They may have three

Cow parsnip has clusters of white flowers.

72

Cow parsnip seed pods.   *Photo by Joy Spurr*

coarsely-toothed leaflets, each of which can be a foot or more across. The leaves are covered with soft white hairs beneath. Clusters of white flowers in compound umbels grow on terminal and axillary stalks. The outermost petals of the marginal flowers are larger than the others. The principal umbel measures from four to eight inches across; a few are larger. After blooming, a large number of flattened, oval seeds appear on the umbels at the top of the plant, which remain on the flowering stalk after the leaves have fallen in late autumn or early winter and is a good identifying feature.

In the field: The best part of the cow parsnip is the edible root, which you can dig from the generally moist soil in which the plant prospers. If it is quite swampy, pull the root by grasping the heavy, hollow stems and tugging it up, but that would be the exception. You will probably need a shovel to extract most of the roots you gather. Peel and boil the root. It has an individual, although not unpleasant taste that seems better when served with mustard or horseradish.

In late spring when the plant is budding or later in the season when the huge umbrellas of flowers appear, gather the flower stalk, which is easily distinguishable from the hollow stem below. Peel and cook or eat it raw, although raw it is sometimes bitter and unpalatable. This solid stalk has a parsnip flavor that some have compared to carrots (although I can never make that connection). It often requires boiling in two waters or more, especially late in the season.

Note the hollow, somewhat hairy stems.

Cow parsnip has another—and somewhat peculiar—use. Collect the broad leaves, burn them over an open fire, and use the ashes as a salt substitute. Otherwise, they have an unbelievably bitter taste when raw. The trace minerals contained in the leaves have a very salty taste, although I haven't the slightest idea what they contain. Their use as a seasoning is apparently quite safe, since many Indian tribes used this exclusively with no harm.

Collecting and burning the leaves is not a lead-pipe cinch, however. Most people who try it usually end up not knowing which ash belongs to the departed leaf and which to the wood that burned it. Two methods don't leave you guessing. A fine wire screen holds the leaves as they burn over the fire without losing the ashes until you are ready to remove and powder them. A less efficient but satisfactory technique is to dry the leaves for a few days, then set them afire on the top of a clean, flat rock. The resulting ashes are ready to powder and use.

It is possible that the leaves and hollow stalks may contain some toxins, but the roots or burned leaves are entirely safe to eat in reasonable quantities. (Before you get a little nervous about that remark, remember that common garden peas are also unhealthy, if eaten in too large a quantity for a long time!)

In the kitchen: The boiled roots, as well as the flower stalks, are best used when including in soups, stews, and other food combinations calling for a flavorful vegetable. You can also use the boiled root as a separate vegetable course. Although I have tried only a few recipes using cow parsnip, you might want to experiment.

SWEET COW PARSNIPS

COW PARSNIP ROOTS
4 cups sliced

SALT

PAPRIKA

BROWN SUGAR *3/4 cup*

LEMON PEEL *1/2 teaspoon grated*

LEMON JUICE *1-1/2 teaspoons*

BUTTER *2 tablespoons*

Boil the roots, sliced into 1-inch pieces, until they are nearly tender. Place them in a shallow, greased baking dish. Season with salt and paprika, then sprinkle the brown sugar over (maple syrup may be substituted). Sprinkle the lemon peel and juice on top and dot with butter. Bake, uncovered, for about 1/2 hour or until tender. Serves 8.

This recipe has an unusual taste. As an interesting variation, add a few slices of apple and some chunk pineapple to the root before adding the brown sugar and lemon.

PARSNIP a la HERCULES

COW PARSNIP STALKS *6*
BUTTER *2 tablespoons*
BOILING WATER *1/2 cup*

SUGAR *1 tablespoon*
SALT *large dash*
LEMON JUICE *1 teaspoon*

Cut the peeled stalks into 1/4-inch cubes. Put in a saucepan with all the other ingredients. Cook over high heat until the water evaporates, keeping tightly covered all the while. Lower the heat and let the stalks brown in the butter. This dish is simple but delicious. Serves 4.

OL' BESSIE'S SURPRISE

COW PARSNIP ROOTS
1 cup cubed

COW PARSNIP STEMS
1 cup peeled and sliced

BUTTER *1 tablespoon*

CHIVES *1 tablespoon chopped*
EGG YOLK *1*
SALT *and* PEPPER
VEGETABLE FILLING
PARSLEY *or* WILD MINT

Cut the roots into 1/2-inch cubes. Peel the stem and cut into 1/2-inch pieces. Boil the 2 together until very soft. Pour off the water and add the butter, chives, and egg yolk. Season to taste. Put over low heat and stir vigorously until the mixture has the consistency of mashed potatoes. Serve by making a reservoir in the center of the dish and filling with freshly boiled pearl onions, garden peas, or boiled camas lily bulbs. Garnish with sprigs of parsley or wild mint. Serves 4.

At first glance, the cow parsnip is not one of the best wild edibles. In the fishing camp or along the trail it is plain and drab, but with a little imagination and effort, it could well become one of your favorites!

DANDELION *(Taraxacum officinale)*

Anyone who can't recognize the common dandelion must have spent his life in a desert or on the moon. In fact, the dandelion has even been found on the margins of desert waterholes! Although this incredibly prolific weed is the nemesis of the gardener and greenskeeper, the fact that some people actually buy seeds and cultivate it speaks well for its acceptance.

The dandelion is rivaled only by the cattail in its distribution and utility. In both cases, there is hardly a part of the plant that is not excellent.

The dandelion has a history as an edible that goes back nearly as far as that of civilization—and perhaps even farther. It was regularly used in the days of the Roman Empire, although it has not been a cultivated plant until recent times. Considering the staggering distribution of the dandelion, there is a serious question whether it *needed* cultivation! The cultivated plants have much larger leaves and not so much of the white, milky fluid that makes the plant bitter in the fall.

Someone in the recesses of history likened the sharply toothed leaves of the dandelion to a lion's tooth, hence the name. In Roman times it was called

Even though this dandelion has already bloomed, the smaller inside leaves will make excellent greens.

DANDELION *(Taraxacum officinale)*

"Dens-leonis," literally "lion's teeth." Even though most of us have a little trouble making the connection, the name stuck.

None of the species found here are sufficiently different to rate special mention. All are equally palatable. There are even a couple of impostors that probably appear in your lawn. One of these is *Hypochoeris radicata,* or hairy cat's ear. Like the dandelion, it grows from a basal rosette of leaves and yields a bright yellow head of many linear petals backed by a green bract (really an involucre, or large group of bracts). Cat's ear leaves are considerably hairier than those of the dandelion, but I have eaten them and found them identical to those of the dandelion, except for the hairs.

There is another plant that looks slightly like a dandelion, at least for a few weeks in spring. It is the tansy ragwort, a noxious weed that is becoming a real problem. I've included a picture so you can see the much finer toothing and indentation of its leaves. It is hard to confuse the two, but get to know tansy ragwort so you can remove it wherever you find it. This bitter-tasting

Tansy ragwort,
a noxious weed.

A large first year dandelion root, suitable as a potherb.

plant is not highly poisonous but all portions of the plant are potentially dangerous. It is reported to contain six different alkaloid poisons. It is a menace to dairymen, as cattle may eat it if other more palatable plants are not available and accumulate a build-up of poisonous alkaloids. Some states now have full-scale programs under way to eliminate this pest, but the tansy ragwort seems to be spreading in spite of efforts to eradicate it.

Not only is the common dandelion versatile and delicious, any way you look at it, among the collectible wide edible plants, it is a dandy!

Habitat and distribution: With the exception of barren desert or the polar regions, the dandelion is found in almost any kind of soil in all climates throughout the continent. It is probably the most widespread and abundant weed in the world.

Description: This common, well-known plant is an annual or sometimes biennial that has a rosette or cluster of basal leaves that are deeply cleft along both sides. A hollow stem supports the brilliant head of yellow flowers. In the summer the flower becomes a rounded, soft head of downlike tufts that bear

Older dandelion roots.

the tiny seeds as they are blown by the wind. A heavy, carrot-shaped root supports the plant.

In the field: Pick young dandelion leaves and eat them raw or in a salad combined with other greens, or blanched for a winter salad. Boil the older leaves, usually in two waters, to remove a bitter taste that increases as the leaf ages. You can also use young leaves as a cooked green. Try freezing partially cooked leaves for later use.

The bright yellow flowers are edible, but acrid in taste. Use them as the basis for a popular sweet wine or steeped into a refreshing tea.

Boil the roots as a potherb, but first peel them, as much of the bitterness is in the skin. Older roots have a series of veins around a central core that emits the bitter, milky fluid when cut, so cook the roots in several changes of water if they are to be eaten.

Because of the characteristic bitterness of the roots, they are an excellent coffee substitute in the field. Chop the pared roots into small pieces and roast them, then brew as any coffee. There is little difference in the flavor of dandelion coffee and the coffee bean.

In the kitchen: Anyone who has ever cooked spinach, chard, or any other leafy vegetable knows what to do with dandelion: use it the same as any other leafy green plant. The ways to use dandelion are virtually endless, and the flavor is unlike any other. It is an excellent salad green, except when the plant is old and the leaves contain the bitter sap. For salads, pick the leaves before a flower appears.

DANDY CHICKEN CASSEROLE

DANDELION GREENS
3 cups chopped

BUTTER *3 tablespoons*

FLOUR *1/4 cup*

SALT

MILK *2 cups*

PARMESAN CHEESE
3 tablespoons grated

LEMON JUICE *1 tablespoon*

DILL WEED *pinch*

CHICKEN *6 ounces, boned and chopped*

PARMESAN CHEESE

WHOLE WHEAT BISCUITS *or* HOMEMADE BREAD

Boil dandelion greens well. In a saucepan melt the butter and stir in flour and a little salt. Blend in the milk and cook, stirring thoroughly, until the mixture is thick and bubbly. Add Parmesan cheese, lemon juice, and dill. Remove from heat and stir in the drained dandelion greens and chicken. Turn into a greased 1-quart casserole. Sprinkle with a little Parmesan cheese and bake at 375° for 25 minutes. Serve over whole wheat biscuits or thick chunks of homemade bread. This hot and hearty dish is a meal in itself. Serves 6.

Just to prove how much fun foraging can be and how delicious you can make it, try this superb chowder.

CRAWDADDY DANDY

DANDELION ROOTS *1 cup pared and diced*

CRAWFISH TAILS *1 cup boiled*

MILK *3 cups*

BUTTER *2 tablespoons*

CATTAIL SHOOTS *1/2 cup cut into round slices*

WILD ONION *1/4 cup chopped*

SALT *and* PEPPER

BUTTER

Boil the dandelion roots in fresh water. Shell the boiled crawfish tails and set aside. Boil the dandelion roots in a second fresh water. Drain and boil a third time. Meanwhile, heat the milk to almost boiling. After the roots boil the third time, saute them along with the crawfish tails in butter in a large saucepan. When they have just begun to brown, pour roots, crawfish tails, and butter all into the hot milk. Reduce the heat and stir in the cattail shoots and onion. Season to taste with salt and freshly ground pepper. Serve with a pat of butter in the middle of each piping hot bowl. Serves 6.

This rich, creamy soup is heady stuff—you'll be hooked forever!

CLASSIC DANDELION SALAD

DANDELION GREENS *1 pound*
MEDIUM ONION *1, chopped*
RADISHES *12*
MEDIUM CUCUMBER
1, pared and sliced

WHOLE EGGS *2, hard-boiled*
SHARP CHEDDAR CHEESE
in thin strips
MINT SPRIG *and* RIPE OLIVES
DRESSING *or* LEMON WEDGES

Rinse the dandelion greens and chill in the refrigerator until ready to combine the salad. In a large salad bowl, combine the dandelion, onion, and radishes, sliced into thin rounds. Put about half the cucumber in with this and toss lightly. Put alternating slices of egg and cucumber around the margin and arrange the cheese strips in spokes about the center. Garnish with a sprig of mint in the center and a few ripe olives. Serve with a choice dressing or fresh lemon wedges. Serves 4.

CREAMED DANDELION GREENS

DANDELION GREENS *about 3 cups*
BUTTER *2 tablespoons*
FLOUR *2 tablespoons*
MILK *or* CREAM *1 cup*

PEARL ONIONS *1 cup*
DRY SHERRY *1 teaspoon*
ALMONDS

Boil the dandelion greens in fresh water while you prepare the white sauce. To make the sauce, melt butter over low heat in a large saucepan and add the flour gradually, stirring well. Slowly stir in the milk or cream until you have a smooth, rich sauce. Add the cooked greens, raw onion, and sherry and simmer for 15 minutes or until the onions are done. Garnish with sliced almonds. This is a delicious, colorful dish that brings out the finest flavor of the young dandelion leaves. They are especially attractive if you slice them lengthwise before boiling. Serve with any meat or fish main dish. Serves 6.

GRANDPA'S GREEN IRISH SOUP

DANDELION GREENS
1 quart chopped

BUTTER *2 tablespoons*
FLOUR *3 tablespoons*
MILK *2 cups*

ONION *1/4 cup chopped*
RICE *1/2 cup cooked*
SALT *and* PEPPER
PARSLEY

Chop the dandelion greens into 1/2-inch strips and boil in fresh water. In a large saucepan, melt the butter over low heat and stir in the flour. Be careful not to burn the flour. Add the milk and allow to come nearly to a boil. Into this stir the onion, rice, and boiled greens. Simmer for about 15 minutes, until the soup takes on a pastel green color and the onion is transparent. Season to taste and serve with hard crackers and a garnish of parsley sprigs. Serves 6.

Made with either dandelion or nettles, this soup was a favorite in western soft-coal towns around the turn of the century.

DEVIL'S CLUB *(Oplopanax horridum)*

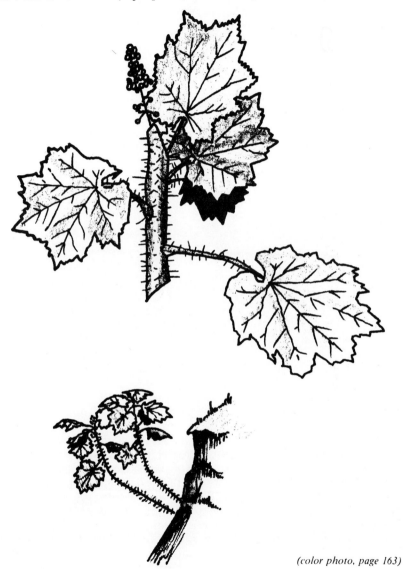

(color photo, page 163)

A gust of wind lifts the ferocious leaf, revealing the sharp spines.

Although devil's club is not found in many places, it is abundant in those areas that favor its growth. As the scientific name implies, the plant is something on the order of horrible and has long been the bane of woodsmen who must cross the steep, damp stream banks it calls home. The stalk, stems, and leaves carry long yellow thorns that are barbed and very sharp. A devil's club thorn, if untended, can work its way through a finger and emerge—after much pain and infection—on the side opposite its entry. Many loggers and travelers have received painful wounds from grasping the heavy stalk as they slipped on the mossy rocks of its typical habitat.

It's hard to imagine that a plant so malevolent could be edible, and the fact is, only the tender new shoots, available for two or three weeks each year, are ever used for food. Many coastal Indian tribes eagerly dug for these shoots. They are tender, sweet, and very tasty. The roots were chewed for their flavor but were too tough to be swallowed, even after prolonged boiling.

Devil's club roots were traded to traveling Indian bands who carried them to the plains east of the Cascades, where they brought a high price as a medicinal preparation. There is some basis for such use, since devil's club is a member of the ginseng family. (Ginseng root, the basis of some modern medicines, brings very high prices today.)

Include devil's club in your foraging expedition for its novelty and the excellent flavor of the cooked shoot.

Habitat and distribution: Devil's club frequents rocky, moss-covered stream banks along the Pacific coast from central Oregon as far north as Alaska. A few specimens of a closely related plant have been reported in northern California, but the plant is extremely rare there.

Description: The light brown stems rise from the moss in crooks and twists and are covered with long yellow spines. Several smaller annual stems support the large maple-shaped leaves, flower clusters, and berries. All above-ground parts of the plant except the flowers and berries are spiny and dangerous. The leaves are up to 18 inches across and are coarsely lobed and finely toothed. From above, the pale green leaves closely resemble a large

Note the oddly twisted trunk.

In the darkness of the damp forest, the devil's club leaves grow in a horizontal plane.

maple, but below, the many evil spines protruding from the veins make the distinction quite clear. The overall covering of spines and the oddly twisted, often horizontal trunk are the best keys to identification.

Devil's club bears large clusters of bright red berries in the fall months, but they are not edible. Their taste is reported to be terrible, and they contain varying amounts of toxins. It is unlikely that anyone would eat enough to prove fatal because of the bad taste, but don't experiment with them.

In the field: Despite the fact that devil's club is a difficult, dangerous plant to handle, collecting roots and shoots is easy. Near the bottom of the stalk or just below the moss surface, the spines disappear. Tug upward on the root and it will tear through the moss for several feet, exposing the unguarded portion and the several young shoots. They are smooth and easy to snap off the main root. The shoots remain edible until the first traces of the yellow spines appear. Lightly boil them in salted water and they will retain a tender yet crisp character. Peel the tough, brownish-yellow skin from the roots, which you can chew for their refreshing flavor.

In the kitchen: Because devil's club shoots retain crispness after boiling, they are excellent for chilling, slicing, and adding to a salad to bring a great new flavor to a humdrum first course.

In spite of its limitations of range and season, devil's club has long been a popular food among hiking parties and survey crews. Adapt this backpacker's recipe to your kitchen.

HELLZAPOPPIN

BEEF JERKY *about 1 cup sliced*
DEVIL'S CLUB SHOOTS *2 cups cut into 1-inch lengths*
CATTAIL ROOTS *1 cup pared and sliced*
SALT *and* PEPPER

Put the jerky, cut into short pieces, into boiling water. Drop in the devil's club and cattail roots; season to taste. (Potatoes may be substituted for cattail, which usually grows somewhere near devil's club.) This dish makes the jerky almost tasty and is excellent after it simmers for about 1/2 hour. Reserve the broth for a fine soup stock. Serves 8.

DEER 'n' DEVIL'S DELIGHT

DEVIL'S CLUB SHOOTS *1 cup*
SMALL VENISON STEAKS *4*
ONION *1/4 cup chopped*
MUSHROOMS *1/2 cup sliced*
BUTTER *2 tablespoons*
FLOUR *3 tablespoons*
MILK *1/2 cup*
SALT *and* PEPPER

Boil the devil's club shoots and cut into 1/2 inch pieces. Set aside. In a heavy skillet, fry the venison steaks until they are well done. As they fry, in a separate skillet, saute the devil's club shoots, onion, and mushroom in the butter. Once they are brown, cover and lower the heat so the butter steams into these vegetables. Remove the steaks from the skillet and place in a warming pan while you add the flour to the venison fat, stirring constantly. Slowly stir in the milk until you have a rich natural gravy. Season to taste. Serves 4.

Arrange the steak on each plate, then spoon the sauteed vegetables alongside. Pour a wide stripe of the gravy over both the meat and vegetables. The combination of succulent onion, crisp devil's club, and delicate mushrooms are an unmatched complement to your wild venison.

Once you taste devil's club, you'll eagerly await the coming of spring, when the young shoots begin to show. Devil's club is a much-maligned plant and probably deserves it, but is not without redeeming virtue!

DOCK *(Rumex crispus* and related species)

Another of the very common weeds, dock exists in one of a dozen or so forms, all of which are edible and delightful. *Rumex crispus* or *R. hymenosepalus* are the most common and the tastiest.

Characterized by a tall central spike containing many coffee-colored seeds, dock is locally called Indian coffee, Indian tobacco, or any of several other names. (The seeds are no good for coffee, or for smoking either!)

Although it was long known as wild rhubarb, the two are not related. While the common rhubarb stems are edible, their leaves are poisonous, and several cases of human death have been attributed to eating them. Fortunately dock leaves and stems are quite safe.

Dock

DOCK *(Rumex crispus)*

The lumpy look of the large young leaves is a good identifier.

As with many foods, it is possible that eating great quantities could bring on some kind of illness from accumulated poisons, but it is hardly likely that anyone could eat enough for that. Dock is served regularly in my home simply because we enjoy the asparagus flavor. (My side yard, which harbors dock, dandelion, and plantain in quantity, is left unmowed as a hedge against high food costs and a generally unproductive garden plot!)

American Indians ate all the docks and the early settlers used them widely to augment their meager foodstuffs. A journal entry from a settler near Oakville, Washington, in the mid-1800s notes that curly dock was the first green vegetable the party ate after several weeks of cross-country travel. They found it "attractive to the taste," an opinion repeated often in modern times.

Habitat and distribution: Dock is found in one form or another in virtually all parts except the deserts. It also ranges across the entire United States and the southern half of Canada. In nearly all areas you find one of the two more popular species, especially on both seaboards, where several varieties thrive. Dock prefers light, poor soil and doesn't require much water.

Description: The various *Rumex* species have dark green leaves that are smooth-edged, wavy, or crisped and sheath the rather succulent stem. The stem and leaves are green, tinged with red, and may often be strongly red-tinged. All species have coarse ribbed stems that bear clusters of brown to nearly black fruits at or near the top. Many of the plants are 24 inches tall or more. The leaves have rather deep and reticulated veins, giving the leaf a "lumpy" appearance. When open, the flowers are brownish and in clusters. The fruits, upon close examination, are three-angled and veiny.

In the field: Simply pick the leaves and stems of the plant, tear away the brown spots, and boil the cleaned leaves. It is simpler to cook and eat if you cut the plant into one- to two-inch strips.

When the plant reaches maturity, the basal leaves are quite large and are borne on thick stems. These make a good substitute for rhubarb in a pie. As the plant ages, it begins to pick up a somewhat acid taste and may require boiling in two waters before it is really good. The cooked young leaves take on the pastel green of cooked asparagus, and the taste is quite similar.

The roots contain large amounts of tannic acid, so don't eat them. Some Indian tribes dried the roots and steeped them into a tea as a cold remedy, but that use is discouraged. Individual plants may have tannin contents high enough to be dangerous or cause an allergic reaction. (Incidentally, effort has been made to hybridize some dock varieties as a commercial source of tannic acid.)

To prepare this plant for cooking, stack the leaves and slice into inch-wide strips.

In the kitchen: In spring dock is among the lightest, tastiest of all cooked greens. It has gained wide acceptance as a potherb, particularly in green casseroles and one-dish meals. My family vastly prefers it as a simple cooked green, often covered with a zesty cheese sauce or hollandaise.

DRAGON'S-EYED DOCK

DOCK LEAVES *and* STEMS *1/2 pound*	BACON DRIPPINGS *1 tablespoon*
RED PEPPERS *2 tablespoons chopped*	LEMON JUICE *2 tablespoons* WHOLE EGGS *2, hard-boiled*
ONION *2 tablespoons chopped*	

Cut the dock into 1/2 inch strips and boil for 5 minutes. Meanwhile, saute the pepper and onion together in the bacon drippings. Drain the dock and stir in the peppers, onion drippings, and lemon juice. Cover and steam over low heat a few minutes until dock is tender. Arrange so a slice of hard-boiled egg peeks up from each serving. This is a colorful gourmet treat. Serves 6.

On an afternoon of successful fishing, you can get most of the ingredients for the following complete dinner by just prowling around the pond or stream bank and collecting what you need.

WUTSUP DOCK DINNER

CATTAIL ROOTS *2 pounds*	OIL
CATTAIL SHOOTS *1/2 cup sliced*	SALT *and* PEPPER
DOCK LEAVES *1/2 pound*	PARSLEY
SMALL WILD ONIONS *3*	LEMON WEDGES
SMALL TROUT *or* PERCH *4*	

Boil the pared and cut-up cattail roots for 1/2 hour or until tender; prepare for mashing. Slice the cattail shoots into thin rounds, the dock into 1/2 inch pieces, and the onion thin. Boil these 3 together for just 5 minutes. Fry the trout until crisp and brown on both sides. Season all 3 dishes to taste. Serves 4.

In the center of a platter, arrange a bed of the dock, onion, and shoot combination. Arrange the mashed cattail roots as a wall around the greens, then place the trout over the soft green bed. Garnish with parsley and lemon wedges. This is a full, delicious meal that can be had for free on a pleasant spring afternoon.

DOUGLAS FIR *(Pseudotsuga menziesii)*
HEMLOCK *(Tsuga heterophylla)*

DOUGLAS FIR *(Pseudotsuga menziesii)*

The Douglas fir and the hemlock are less wild edibles than wild drinkables. I have included them for the fun of thinking about a 200-ton wild edible!

Douglas fir

Although there are a large number of needled conifers, these are the only two widely used as tea sources. Other trees are either unpalatable or unsafe for boiling or steeping. Cedar, for example, releases a rather aromatic oil that has been found unsafe for consumption. But many of the trees have some use and are listed elsewhere in this guide.

On rainy, cold days in the winter, many survey or trail parties build a warming fire to drive off the chill at lunchtime. It isn't unusual to see a can of water sitting in the coals with a handful of fir needles floating on top, while the crew wait for their tea to steep—a fine pick-me-up for a dreary day.

Drink the tea of fir or hemlock (don't forget, we're talking about the hemlock *tree,* not one of the plants named hemlock!) for the sheer taste and pleasure it provides.

Habitat and distribution: DOUGLAS FIR is largely restricted to the Pacific Northwest, and is the tree most seen by people traveling through our conifer forests. Some occur in limited stands along the northern tier of western states. It is often found mixed with other conifers.

Mountain or WESTERN HEMLOCK is found in essentially the same range as the Douglas fir, but not so far to the east. It usually prefers damp shade under the cover of larger conifers.

Description: The giant of the northwest forests, DOUGLAS FIR, is best identified by its cones, which have a three-toothed bract extending from under each scale. The leaves are spirally arranged around the stems. The sharp-pointed leaves, or needles, about an inch long, are fairly soft to the touch, not prickly as in the spruces. The cones hang in clusters or singly; they are two to four inches long.

HEMLOCK *(Tsuga heterophylla)*

Hemlock

WESTERN HEMLOCK is best identified by its drooping top which appears on all trees, regardless of size. The blunted needles are about one-half-inch long and are more or less opposite on the stem. Young stems from which leaves have been shed are rough to the touch due to the persistent leaf bases. The underside has two tiny white lines that run the length of the needle—a good character for identification purposes. The rounded cones hang and are seldom over one-half-inch long.

In the field: Both trees make excellent teas when the needles are steeped in boiling water for a few minutes. Hemlock tea smells a lot like gin—but if you expect the same taste and effect, forget it. Gather a handful of new needles from a young tree (unless you can reach 200 feet) and drop them in boiling water. Allow them to steep for a few minutes to make a heady, aromatic tea. It is best made with clear springwater.

In the kitchen: Just the same as in the field!

FALSE SOLOMON'S SEAL *(Smilacina racemosa)*

The characteristic reclining angle is one of the identification keys to false Solomon's seal.

False Solomon's seal is a strikingly beautiful plant. Early in the written history of the United States this plant appeared as both food and medicine for several bands of Indians in Georgia, Alabama, and Mississippi. Records indicate many western tribes used it sparingly, usually for medicinal purposes. The flavorful roots were often reserved for use in certain religious ceremonies. The journals of Lewis and Clark mention the plant, then called Spikenard, as being used by many tribes from the upper Mississippi River westward to the Columbia. They purchased false Solomon's seal and arrowhead roots from a group along the lower Columbia.

In modern times those interested in wild edibles have largely overlooked false Solomon's seal, simply because it takes quite a bit of preparation. You can use young shoots as a simple potherb without much preparation, but they are very small and have probably been overlooked because many other plants are available at the same time that take less time and effort to collect. Their flavor is neither overpowering nor particularly distinctive.

Habitat and distribution: False Solomon's seal is found in moist ground, generally under the canopy of a conifer growth, although it is also found under old hardwoods, especially in the East. It ranges across the United States and Canada from coast to coast and is absent only from the dry southwestern states.

False Solomon's seal also has the distinct drawback that it can be mistaken for Indian hellebore *(Veratrum viride)* or false white hellebore *(V. californicum),* both of which contain powerful poisons in the roots and young shoots and are not edible. There are two major distinguishing differences between false Solomon's seal and the hellebores.

Description: False Solomon's seal always has a single unbranched stem which terminates either in a 5- to 20-simple-flowered cluster or in many-flowered clusters forming a compound arrangement. Each of the tiny creamy white flowers is composed of a starlike ray of very narrow petals. The white or yellowish flowers of the hellebores have six petals that are broad in relation to their tiny size. False Solomon's seal leaves, up to eight inches long, are alternate and clasp the stem. The hellebores have leaves alternately whorled around the plant, growing from a vertical stalk. (Both photographs are included here to make the distinction clear.) The deeply etched parallel veins are a striking feature of false Solomon's seal, which can attain heights to three feet. The root stalk is quite heavy and twisted, with very thick, fleshy root hairs. The plant reclines at an angle of about 30 degrees from the horizontal even when very young, while the hellebores are very straight, upright plants. In the fall it produces a reddish berry with showy purple spots.

The poisonous hellebore.

The root stalk of false Solomon's seal has many thick, fleshy root hairs.

In the field: Pick young shoots and boil as a potherb with other foods in soups and stews. Dig up the aromatic root and peel it. Soak it in a lye solution of approximately one-half cup of ash lye to one gallon of water for about 24 hours to remove the bitterness and somewhat dull the perfumy flavor, then parboil it to remove the lye. After this process, the root cooked as a starchy vegetable goes well in stews. Also try pickling it, thus preserving the root for use as an appetizer, or include it as an ingredient in a wild relish.

Most authorities agree that the rather bland berries are edible raw, but at least one recognized and respected source has determined that they have a purgative effect if used in quantity. The historic use of the berries for medicinal purposes tends to bear out this contention, so eat them sparingly. The unusual mottled berries have one or two seeds, making their consumption something of a chore anyway!

False Solomon's seal always has a single unbranched stem.

In the kitchen: Flavor and uniqueness are the justifications for trying this showy plant. I have no recipes using false Solomon's seal as a main ingredient. I tend to think of it as a minor, but very flavorful, part of a soup or stew. The taste, however, takes a little getting used to. The most recent roots that I collected were not nearly as overpowering as some earlier specimens, and I believe I could have prepared them without the long soak in lye. Probably a boiling in several changes of water would have made them quite palatable.

I have eaten a few of the berries and found them quite good without suffering any loosening of the inner systems, but I hesitate to make a jam or jelly after a childhood experience with cascara berries that I shall never forget!

For want of a recipe, I plan to do a bit of experimenting in my kitchen. You may be adventurous enough to do the same.

FERNS
BRACKEN FERN *(Pteridium aquilinum)*
DEER FERN *(Blechnum spicant)*
LADY FERN *(Athyrium filix-femina)*
LICORICE FERN *(Polypodium* species*)*
SWORD FERN *(Polystichum munitum)*

There are many fern types growing throughout, and all are reported to be edible in one form or another. Of these, the five listed are the most widespread and have the best possible use as foodstuffs.

Native communities once used all the ferns as a food, but many were not terribly popular, probably because they took more work to prepare. Bracken fern was the most widely used of the five listed, being the easiest to collect and prepare and the most flavorful.

If there is one similarity among all the ferns it is that the mature plant above ground is never used as food. The young sprout, generally called a fiddlehead, is the only exposed part that you can safely eat, although the rhizomes (a modified underground stem) continue to be edible regardless of the age of the plant. Many varieties, when mature, contain small amounts of

A large, mature bracken fern.

BRACKEN FERN *(Pteridium aquilinum)*

This is about as large as a young bracken fern shoot should be for eating—before any traces of open leaves appear.

toxins. It is doubtful that a person would eat enough to cause a serious problem, but instances of poisoning have been noted in grazing stock that consumed inordinate amounts of leafy fern foliage.

BRACKEN FERN is the most widely distributed fern in North America, ranging generally across every climate and region except the deserts. Sparse in some areas, it virtually takes over in others. It is especially dominant in forested, burned-over, and cultivated land.

A major difference between bracken and other ferns is that it does not grow in clusters, but a single leaf grows from an elongate, branching rhizome. The round solid stalk branches into several limbs, a definite departure from the shape of other ferns.

Sori, or spore packets, line the margins of the back of the leaves. The leaves are compound, composed of a large number of leaflets. The black rhizome is usually pulled directly from the ground with little effort.

The best part of the bracken fern is the tender young shoot. Pick the fiddleheads well before any vestiges of open leaves appear. At this stage they are crisp, yet tender, and have a unique flavor. They are fuzzy and often have a rather bulbous head. A little salt in the boiling water improves their flavor.

A young bracken fern shoot.

LADY FERN *(Athyrium filix-femina)*

The rhizomes of the older bracken are quite starchy and tasty—and tougher than nails. The old Indian method of cooking the rhizome was to boil it for about half an hour, then pound it between two flat stones. This separates the tender inner core from the tough vertical fibers, and the starchy mass is eaten as is or dried for future use. After the pounding process, the soft, almost liquid root core makes an excellent thickening ingredient for soups and stews.

WARNING: Recent studies indicate that the tender young bracken shoots should not be eaten because they contain harmful substances that appear to be carcinogenic. Try them at your own risk.

The lazy fronds of LADY FERN are among the most beautiful of all the ferns you'll find. Growing from a short stout rhizome that is densely surrounded by the dark leaf bases of previous years, the slender stems curl back and outward, making a soft green rosette on the forest floor. Most often

The fronds of lady fern appear similar to bracken at first glance.

associated with moist forests, lady fern is usually limited to the northern and coastal regions. Several similar varieties occurring in other areas are used in the same manner. Notable among these is the ostrich fern *(Matteuccia struthiopteris).*

The lady fern (and associated types) is distinguished by its vaselike tufted leaves that pinnately dissect into numerous toothed leaflets. The upper leaflets produce spores scattered on the back sides. The fiddleheads, which arise from the rhizome, are quite small and fuzzy and are loosely covered with transparent brown scales near the base. Gather the fiddleheads by merely plucking them off at the base, rub them briskly between your palms to remove the brown skins and fuzzy hairs, and eat them. They are excellent raw and have a distinct flavor when cooked. Boil them for quite a while until they are as tender as asparagus.

Although edible, disregard the large rhizome as a practical food. Not only are they small and hard to clean, but they taste like a mouthful of shingle nails. The fiddleheads, on the other hand, are a delight when served as a steaming vegetable, topped with a rich cheese dressing.

The delicate little LICORICE FERN is less a major edible than a delightful flavoring. As the name suggests, it has the distinctive flavor of licorice. Many youngsters have enjoyed chewing on a raw piece of rhizome they've just picked from the moss that covers an old maple tree.

A clear identifying feature of the licorice fern is its habitat. This tiny fern never grows in direct soil. Rather, it establishes an intricate rhizome system in the deep moss that covers large maples, rocks, or downed logs, where it often grows in profusion. Nine times out of ten, it is found on the standing trunk of a

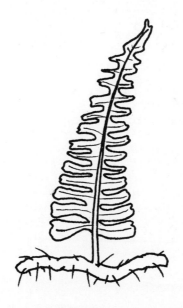

LICORICE FERN *(Polypodium vulgare)*

maple. Since the moss layer must be thick, the licorice fern grows only in the damp climate of the deep forest or stream bank.

Tough brown scales sparsely cover the light green rhizome. The long stiff stems and the deeply-lobed single compound leaf create the appearance of a number of alternate leaflets. The dark brown sori on the underside are large.

Collecting the rhizomes is simple. Pull away a mass of moss at the base of the stem, and the rhizome becomes obvious. It is usually about a quarter-inch in diameter and may be several inches long.

The most refreshing way to enjoy the licorice rhizome is to chew it raw for a few minutes. An immediate bitter taste soon gives way to the incredible sweetness of the licorice for which the plant is named.

A licorice fern growing in the moss of an old maple.

Licorice fern rhizome.

Make a refreshing drink by paring the green skin off the tough rhizome and steeping the chips of skin for a few minutes in hot water. It is more a hot licorice drink than a tea. Use the drink, when cooled, as an interesting flavoring to be mixed in a blackberry jelly or some other dessert. One note of caution—don't boil the pared chips, but steep them in water that has been removed from the heat. I've found that boiling them releases a bitterness from the white pulp that makes the drink unpalatable.

Lest you think this plant's use too limited, I'd like to remind you that imagination goes a long way. A young logger I once knew would brew up a quart or so of this licorice "tea" and store it in a jar under the bunkhouse. In the evening, he'd mix it half-and-half with vodka and claimed it was the finest use he had ever found for either of the liquids. It must have been effective, because the vodka he bought would have eaten the paint off the cook-shack table!

Note the tall waving fronds that stand above the rest of the deer fern.

The source of the DEER FERN's name is obvious. It is a favored food for deer and elk, especially in Washington's Olympic National Forest. Although this fern is largely limited to the coastal forests from northern California to the Alaska panhandle, it is abundant there.

Deer fern was sometimes used as a field food for Indian hunting parties but never gained much popularity in their communities. Other food was available that was much easier to gather and had a better flavor. Even though both the fiddleheads and rhizomes are edible, they have the disadvantage of being rather small — it takes quite a while to collect enough for a family dinner. Moreover, the rhizome is so tough that it requires pounding to free the starchy mass from the fibers.

One of the most distinctive identifying features of the deer fern, especially when compared with the sword fern, is the tall waving fronds that stand far above the rest of the plant. These fertile fronds, usually three or four in number, carry the spores that ensure continuation of the species. The infertile fronds grow in a thick rosette around the rhizome. They tend to taper from the middle toward both ends and are composed of a large number of opposite or offset leaflets. The lower fronds have a conspicuous absence of spores and their leaflets are much wider than those of the fertile fronds.

The fiddlehead should be considered the only edible part of the deer fern, since the rhizomes are highly impractical as anything but a survival food of the last resort. The dainty little fiddleheads are similar to most others, complete with the papery brown base covering and the heavy fuzz that coats them. They are difficult to clean. I prefer them raw, and then usually only when I am sitting amidst a large patch on a rest stop along the trail. To idly pick, clean, and eat these little morsels is a recreation of the first degree. Their nutty flavor is most pleasant and unusual. Think of them as one of nature's finest confections.

DEER FERN *(Blechnum spicant)*

Of all the single-bladed ferns, the SWORD FERN must reign as the numerical monarch, growing in almost any damp, shady forest from sea level to the summer snow line. The clumps of fronds are a familiar sight to anyone who has ever strayed from the roadside, and to most of those who haven't. It is found just about anywhere except the arid and desert sections.

Sword fern was widely used as a food by western Indians but never gained favor with early white settlers, and it soon fell from the list of common edibles. A few recent books have even suggested that the sword fern has some poisonous properties, an observation that may have been based on the mature leaf, which probably *does* contain some toxin, as do nearly all other ferns. Experiments by the U.S. Department of Agriculture indicate that a cow may become ill after eating from 20 to 24 pounds per day for at least 30 days. (If a human ate 20 pounds of *anything* every day, he'd have a good reason for getting sick!) The delicious young fiddleheads are safe in any quantity. They have the unique, admirable quality of maintaining their nutlike flavor even after they are boiled for half an hour.

The sword fern is similar in appearance to the deer fern, but is a larger and coarser plant. The fertile fronds are not elevated but are among the single level of stems that surround the root core. Nearly all the fronds bear the scaly

Sword fern

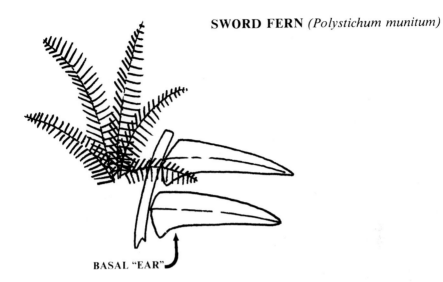

SWORD FERN *(Polystichum munitum)*

BASAL "EAR"

brown spores. The distinguishing key to the sword fern is that each leaf is composed of many individual leaflets, each bearing a pronounced lobe at the base (which shows clearly in the identification drawing).

The rhizome is large enough to be practical as a food, but it still takes a good deal of preparation before boiling and a lot of pounding afterward to remove the incredibly tough fibers. The rhizome, sometimes a foot in diameter, is hard to dig up since it is often intertwined with nearby plants.

The fiddleheads are of respectable size, so just pluck them from the base and rub vigorously to remove the brown lower skin and fluffy hairs.

Because this fern retains its flavor after cooking, I have a favorite way of fixing it in the field. Take a handful of whole, two-inch fiddleheads and lay them on a piece of foil. Salt them lightly, add a dab of butter, and fold the foil into a sort of cup around them. After adding a couple of teaspoons of water, seal the foil package and place it in the coals of a campfire. After about half an hour, the water has steamed away, leaving the buttery flavor in the fiddleheads. Check your vegetable from time to time to make sure it hasn't cooked dry. When tender, they are often slightly brown on the bottom, and they are just plain fabulous. Served with a piece of open-fire roasted grouse, this is a real treat.

In the kitchen: Use the various fiddleheads in largely the same manner. These recipes won't differentiate between them unless a special type is required to make it work. You can really experiment with the ferns!

TILLAMOOK FIDDLER

FIDDLEHEADS *2 cups*
SALT
BUTTER
ONION *2 tablespoons chopped*

SHARP CHEDDAR CHEESE *1 cup grated*
PARSLEY

Boil the fiddleheads for about 15 minutes in lightly salted water. Drain well and place in a small heat-treated serving dish. Dot copiously with butter. Sprinkle the onions over and cover all with the grated cheddar cheese. Place under the broiler just long enough to thoroughly melt the cheese down through the onion and fiddleheads. Garnish with parsley. Delightful! Serves 4 to 6.

BULLY BRACKEN SOUP

BRACKEN FIDDLEHEADS *2 cups*
SALT
BRACKEN RHIZOMES *36*
SMALL BEEF SOUPBONE
MILK *1-1/2 cups*

WHOLE KERNEL CORN *1/2 cup*
SALT *and* PEPPER
BUTTER
PARSLEY

Boil the fiddleheads in salty water for 20 minutes. Wash in cold water and set aside to dry. Boil the bracken rhizomes for 1-1/2 hours. Pound the rhizomes with a meat hammer and separate the pulp from the fibers by rolling hard with a rolling pin. Put the white pulp in a cup and set aside.

Heat the soupbone in the milk until almost boiling. (Go ahead. It sounds terrible, but the result is great!) Add the fiddleheads and corn and simmer for about 15 minutes. Remove the soupbone and add the rhizome pulp, stirring constantly. Season to taste. Just before serving, run the whole thing through a blender if you desire. It makes the soup creamier. Serve piping hot with a pat of butter and a sprig of parsley floating on the surface. It is a rich, brown soup that you'll really enjoy, despite the work involved. Serves 6.

NECK AND NECK SUPREME

SWORD FERN FIDDLEHEADS *1 cup*
BUTTER *1 tablespoon*
CRACKER CRUMBS *1/2 cup*
CREAM *2 tablespoons*

ONION *2 tablespoons chopped*
CELERY *1/2 cup chopped*
SALT *and* PEPPER
ROCK CORNISH HENS *2*
BUTTER

Boil the sword fern fiddleheads for just 10 minutes. Cut into small pieces. Combine next 6 ingredients in a saucepan over low heat until cooked into a thick dressing. Stuff the game hens with this dressing, rub them with butter, and roast covered or in foil until completely done and tender. The crisp nutty flavor of the fiddleheads makes this simple dressing a dish to remember. (In place of the game hens, a single wild grouse will make this a superior main course. A spoonful of sherry over the bird before roasting is optional and thoroughly recommended.) Serves 4.

FIREWEED *(Epilobium angustifolium)*

(color photo, page 167)

Most people first notice fireweed as a beautiful red or purple flower that covers acre upon acre of wasteland in the summer. I particularly like this lovely plant when it rises from the ashes of a forest fire or slash-burn. It seems to promise that new growth will soon cover the desolate landscape. It very often is the first plant to bloom among the blackened snags, gaining a rapid foothold soon after the fire.

Fireweed, being abundant throughout the country, was widely used as a potherb by early Indians and was soon adopted by white settlers. They recognized this weed from the East and even from Europe, where it was often used for food, especially in poor times.

The dried leaves were historically used in Great Britain to mix with tea, both to change the flavor and to extend the meager supplies of regular tea in the poor man's cottage. Even though tea is no longer the expensive commodity it was then, the tea-loving British still use fireweed to some extent.

Fireweed is certainly not limited to producing tea, being almost entirely edible in a variety of ways. Leaves, shoots, stalks, and even pulp are valuable as substantial foodstuffs. The Indians of the West and Canada used the plant most widely as a potherb, eagerly collecting the young plants and boiling them as a superb green.

Fireweed even filled the bill as a sort of refreshing confection for many Indian parties, who split open the older stalks and scraped out the sticky pith and ate it. It is somewhat glutinous and quite sweet.

Habitat and distribution: Fireweed is very often found in waste or burned-over land (hence the common name) and generally prefers rich, moist soil. It can stand direct sun but is also found in shady areas. It is far more prevalent in the extreme western and northern regions, where there is more moisture than in the drier interior sections.

Description: Fireweed is a tall unbranched plant from about two feet to over six feet high. The leaves are alternate. They may have very tiny teeth but often are virtually smooth, dark green above and whitish-green beneath. The center vein is quite evident, but the smaller veins are minute. The flowers are borne in a tall terminal raceme and are red, magenta, deep pink, or purple. When mature, the hairy seeds are released from the capsules and are carried about in the wind like wispy threads of cotton.

In the field: Eat young shoots and leaves raw in a salad or boil them as a substitute for asparagus, which the unique flavor somewhat resembles. As raw greens, they are good only when very young, becoming somewhat bitter with age.

After you halve the older stalks, scrape out the soft pith. It is an excellent addition to soups and an intriguing sweetener on a rough-ground cereal at breakfast time.

Dry the leaves and steep into a tea that is particularly good when it is chilled and sweetened. Adding a few crushed hemlock needles often improves the hot tea. During steeping, add a sprig of mint, a little honey, or even a small bit of the fireweed's own sweet pith for flavorful variation.

Young fireweed.

In the kitchen: Enjoy fireweed for its fine flavor and ready availability. It is another of those wonders that provide a lot of fun and challenge in the kitchen. If you want to go to the trouble of stripping the leaves from about 40 young plants, try this one.

FIREWEED FANTASY

SWEET FIREWEED PITH *1 cup*　　EGG WHITES *2*
WATER *3 teaspoons*　　WILD STRAWBERRIES
VANILLA *1/4 teaspoon*　　NUTS

Boil the pulp in the 3 teaspoons of water (no more!) until it is very soft and runny. Mix in the vanilla and remove from the heat. Add the 2 egg whites and beat vigorously until it is stiff. Pour over freshly picked wild strawberries and sprinkle with finely chopped nuts. This is perhaps the most delicate, delicious dessert that could ever be made! Serves 8.

NAKED FIREWEED CREAM

ONION *1/4 cup chopped*
MUSHROOMS *1/2 cup sliced*
BUTTER
MILK *2/3 cup*

FLOUR *2 tablespoons*
YOUNG FIREWEED STALKS
1/2 pound
SALT *to taste*

In a saucepan, saute the onion and mushrooms in a little butter, then add the milk and bring almost to a boil. Stir in the flour to make a thin cream sauce (add a little flour to reach the desired consistency, if necessary). Reduce the heat and add the fireweed stalks, cut into 2-inch lengths. Season to taste and simmer until the stalks are tender. Serves 6.

FIREWEED FIESTA

FIREWEED LEAVES *and* STEMS *3 cups*
WATER *1/4 cup*
SOY SAUCE
FRANKFURTERS *1 cup cut up*
GREEN PEPPER *1/4 cup diced*

GREEN ONIONS *2 tablespoons chopped*
WATER CHESTNUTS *2 tablespoons sliced*
MUSHROOMS *1/4 cup sliced*

In a large saucepan, boil the fireweed for about 10 minutes. Drain and add 1/4 cup of fresh water and a dash of soy sauce. Put in the remaining ingredients and simmer covered until the greens are tender. Serves 6.

DUBLIN FIREWEED

CORNED BEEF BRISKET
3-4 pounds

POTATOES *4, pared and halved*
SMALL ONIONS *8*
WATER *4 cups*

DRY WHITE WINE *1 cup*
FIREWEED LEAVES *and* STEMS *2 cups*
SALT *and* PEPPER
MUSTARD *or* HORSERADISH
SAUCE

Cook this 1-pot dinner in 4 stages. First, boil the brisket for 1-1/2 hours, then add the potatoes and onions and continue to boil for another 30 minutes. Drain the meat and vegetables, add 4 cups of water and the wine, and return to the stove until it boils again. Finally, add the fireweed greens, season, cover, and simmer the lot for about 25 minutes. Remove the brisket and serve it on a platter. Serve the drained vegetables in a separate dish, all mixed together. This hearty boiled dinner takes a lot of time, but very little work, and the result is excellent. Serve the meat with a creamy mustard or horseradish sauce. Serves 8.

GOATSBEARD *(Tragopogon dubius)*
OYSTER PLANT, SALSIFY

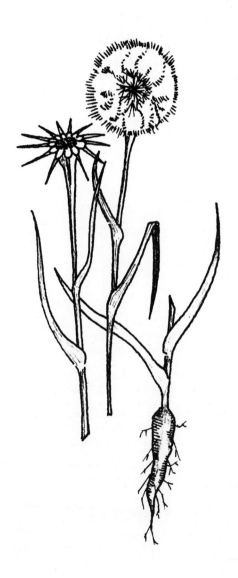

Goatsbeard buds

Goatsbeard is one of the most beautiful of all wildflowers. The delicate flower may be either yellow or a brilliant purple, depending on the variety you find, and is a real show-off among the wildflowers.

The plant has an interesting history, being both an important food and a folk medicine to various cultures in the past. The milky juice was distilled as a sort of antiseptic; pads were soaked in the distillate and placed over open sores.

Pliny recorded the most novel use of goatsbeard. He wrote that the milky sap was mixed with woman's milk and applied to the eyes. It was used for absolutely any disorder of the eyes, taken internally or applied externally. It's doubtful that goatsbeard would get the rousing endorsement of either the medical profession or women's liberation groups.

A variety of goatsbeard, *Tragopogon porrifolius,* is cultivated and is generally called salsify.

Goatsbeard is sometimes known as oyster plant, owing to a flavor that is supposed to resemble oysters. Frankly, I could never make the connection, and my love for oysters is probably surpassed only by my vivid imagination. I tend to equate the flavor with that of cultivated parsnip, but there are definite differences. Personally, I pick goatsbeard over parsnip any time I have the choice.

Goatsbeard has a lot of other redeeming virtues, one of which is the milky sap, which can be allowed to congeal and used as a chewing gum. I'm sure the juice, thus used, has no nutritional value, but it might just clean the coating off your teeth—or your messkit, or your galoshes, or anything it might come in contact with! I hasten to add that it is completely *safe* to use for chewing.

This is another plant that increases in calories if it is stored for a length of time before being used. It has something to do with the conversion of natural sugars into starch after picking, The whole thing is kind of confusing to anyone but a chemist or an agricultural county agent!

Habitat and distribution: Although goatsbeard is found on open waste ground, it prefers the somewhat drier climates usually associated with large grain-producing districts. Some of the varieties are more adaptable to the damper climates, particularly those with yellow flowers. Some are found near the seacoast, but they are generally sparse in such wet areas.

Description: Goatsbeard is easy to recognize by the milky juice exuded from injured stems or leaves. The leaves are long and grasslike, very definitely clasping the stem, often almost surrounding the stalk at the base of the leaf. The center vein is distinct at the back of the leaf. The stem is swollen just below the flower head. The single flower head is bright yellow and raylike. The seeded head resembles a giant dandelion.

The pared root quickly turns brown, owing to a thick sap that flows freely from the core.

In the field: You can often pull the root directly from the ground, but it may require some energetic digging, particularly if the soil is rocky and hard. Pare the fleshy taproot to expose the whitish inner root, and then eat it raw or cooked. It is the raw substance that is supposed to taste like oysters, while the cooked root takes on the sharp taste of cooked parsnip. Actually, it tastes like goatsbeard, and comparisons are pretty fanciful at best.

Pick very young stems and boil them in soups and stews or use as a cooked green. Don't pick them after they reach about six inches high, since the milky latex in the plant isn't at all pleasant to the taste. As a wild edible, it is best to concentrate on the root as a source of enjoyment.

In the kitchen: Goatsbeard has such a distinctive taste that it is best served as an undressed vegetable, seasoned only lightly, if at all. Like the oyster to which it is compared, savor it for its uniqueness of flavor, rather than cover it with stronger tastes. (Personally, I think the guy who fries his oysters to the consistency of an asbestos shingle and then dips them in a fiery tomato-and-pepper sauce should be flogged with a wet carp, and that applies to goatsbeard, too!)

NAKED GOATSBEARD

GOATSBEARD ROOT WATER
1/2 cup per person

Put the pared and sliced root in the water, boil it, and serve—as is.

HORSETAIL *(Equisetum* species)
FOXTAIL, SCOURING RUSH

This is one of the most common wild edibles, occurring in several forms throughout the world. Records indicate that horsetail was used extensively in historic times, dating as far back as the Roman Empire. The plant was apparently cultivated in those days, and the young sprouts were a popular food. Early Indian societies in North America used horsetail widely, and the white settlers and pioneers quickly accepted it.

Note the difference between the fertile and sterile fronds.

Horsetail has a gritty feeling because of the silicon on the surface; hence the popular name scouring rush. It is good for cleaning pots and pans while camping, since the sharp grit of the stem surface cleans and polishes aluminum. A quarter of a century ago my father and I visited a backwoods logging camp in northern California, where I watched the cookhouse swamper scrubbing the ten-gallon cooking pots with handfuls of horsetail. After a hot rinse, they shined like a new penny. Since then, I've used them on my frying pans and tin plates wherever I camp.

Horsetail gets its name from the whorls of wiry branches on the green stems, somewhat resembling a fancied horse's tail. It is an inoffensive weed that seldom invades a lawn or garden. After you try it, it may well gain a bit of respect.

Habitat and distribution: Horsetail is found massed along the margins of creeks, swamps, or lakes; the plant grows profusely in shaded woods, damp soil, or cutover land and roadside embankments. Often you'll find it spread over a couple of miles of roadside. It usually isn't found in the very dry or desert regions.

Description: Horsetails are vertical, rushlike plants that have many small leafless branches growing in whorls around some or all of the stems. The branches effectively take the place of leaves in securing nutrients from sunlight and rain. The stem is jointed at regular intervals, with a ragged crown around the plant at each joint. Fertile fronds, which lack the stiff branches, grow along with the whorled sterile fronds. The roots are usually many-branched and creeping, but in some varieties may be simple rhizomes. Plants vary in size at maturity from about nine inches to over three feet.

In the field: Clip off the young, fertile shoots (those without whorls) at ground level and strip off the outer stem surface—a quick, simple task. The gritty and indigestible silica on the surface must be removed to render the horsetail edible. Then boil the shoots in the same manner as asparagus, to which its flavor is similar.

The starchy rhizome is reputed to be edible but has never been held in high regard. I consider the rhizomes rather small and difficult to clean and cook, and I prefer to deal with only the upper shoot, although the rhizome could be experimented with to determine its usefulness.

The inner pulp of the young shoots is eaten raw and has a sweet, pleasant flavor. It is especially good when combined with a salad that uses the lemony sheep sorrel as a complementary taste.

In the kitchen: Horsetail is a fine vegetable to include with dinner. If the stem surface is peeled away carefully, the result is a compact, attractive plant that rather resembles a prime asparagus spear.

The fertile shoot lacks the whorls of wiry branches.

DAN PATCH ITALIANO

HORSETAIL SPEARS *3 cups*
peeled
BUTTER *1 tablespoon*
ITALIAN SAUSAGE *1/2 cup*
chopped

PARMESAN CHEESE *1/2 cup*
grated

Boil the spears until tender. Drain well and arrange on a heatproof serving dish. Dot with butter and sprinkle the sausage in a strip that covers the center half of the spears. Pour the cheese thickly over the strip of sausage, so that the tips of the horsetail spears remain uncovered. Place under the broiler until the cheese melts through the sausage and spears. Serve as a side dish to a fresh ham or pork roast. Serves 6.

HORSETAIL GUMBO

HORSETAIL SPEARS *1 cup peeled*
ONION *1/4 cup chopped*
BUTTER *1 tablespoon*
FLOUR *2 tablespoons*
TOMATO SAUCE *1-1/2 cups*
WATER *1 cup*
CELERY *1/4 cup*
finely chopped

SMALL SHRIMP *6-1/2-ounce can*
CRABMEAT *4 ounces*
LEMON JUICE *1 tablespoon*
SMALL OYSTERS *6*
LEMON WEDGES
PARSLEY
SALT *and* PEPPER

Boil the horsetail for just 5 minutes. Drain and set aside. Saute the onion in butter and stir in the flour until smooth. Put in a saucepan and add the tomato sauce and 1 cup of water. Add the horsetail spears, celery, shrimp, and crabmeat. Simmer for about 25 minutes, until the horsetail is tender. Stir in the lemon juice and add the oysters. Stir until the oysters are plump and tender, but don't overcook. Garnish this rich main dish with lemon wedges and parsley. (Although the ingredients usually provide all the zest needed, you may wish to season with salt and freshly ground pepper during cooking.) Main course for 4 or side dish for 6 to 8.

SWEET SUMMER SALAD

SHEEP SORREL *1 cup*
MINER'S LETTUCE *1 cup*
WILD ONION *1/4 cup chopped*
CATTAIL SHOOTS *1/2 cup*
sliced

HORSETAIL SPEARS *1/2 cup*
peeled
SALMONBERRIES *about 12*
LEMON *or* SPICY DRESSING

Tear the sorrel and miner's lettuce leaves and mix in the raw onion and cattail shoots. Arrange the raw horsetail spears in spoke fashion over the salad. Dot the salad with colorful salmonberries and serve with a dash of lemon or a spicy dressing. Serves 6.

Generally, these plants can all be found growing together in the springtime or early summer and therefore can all be collected in a few minutes. This is a delightful salad that makes a fine holiday lunch when served with a hearty sandwich and tea.

LABRADOR TEA *(Ledum groenlandicum)*

OLD LEAF

YOUNG LEAF

(color photo, page 163)

As the name implies, this plant is used exclusively for tea. It can hardly be mistaken for any other plant, except the mountain Labrador tea, which can be used in exactly the same way.

Historical writings show that the Pilgrims quickly adopted the traditional Indian use of this plant and began brewing a strong, flavorful tea that they judged to be nearly as good as the Oriental varieties they had in England. The dried leaves do not much resemble tea leaves, but the flavor certainly does.

Habitat and distribution: Labrador tea is found virtually anywhere in the United States and Canada, ranging even to the subarctic regions of the eastern seaboard and into the northern territories of western Canada. It is not found in the semiarid or desert regions, but grows at the margins of mossy bogs and on wetter hillsides at lower and middle elevations. Moutain Labrador tea *(L. glandulosum)* is usually found on moist, rocky slopes from the middle to higher elevations in all but the driest of climates. Both range throughout the North American continent, but may vary widely in abundance.

Description: Labrador tea is a twisted shrub usually about two to four feet high. The young twigs are hairy and have leaves, but the lower stems are usually bare. The leaves are distinctively curled under at the outer margins,

Leaves are curled under at the outer margins.

Labrador tea

giving them a "rolled" effect. The underside is distinguished by a coarse, rusty wool or reddish hairs that help preserve moisture for the leaves. This characteristic is missing from the mountain variety. Even though they are classified as deciduous, there are leaves on the bushes through most of the year, with new growth appearing during a long growing season.

In spring or early summer, a showy head of small white flowers appears at the terminus of the limbs. They dry into a seedy husk that usually remains on the plant until the following season. While the old leaves have a prominent center vein, younger ones have a very distinctive arrangement of three parallel veins, with opposite veins leading away from the outer two (see drawing and photos for positive identification).

In the field: Except in the middle of winter the leaves are easily found. Collect and dry the leaves, crush, and then boil or steep them in hot water to the desired color and strength. As a tea, this plant is as tasty and refreshing as the finest orange or pekoe tea. A dry mint leaf added per cupful as it steeps changes its character to a novel, fragrant delight. Another interesting flavor departure is to drop just a few broken fir needles into the pot.

In the kitchen: Ditto, with sugar and lemon or wild honey.

LAMB'S QUARTERS *(Chenopodium album)*
GOOSEFOOT, PIGWEED

With the possible exception of dandelion, lamb's quarters, often known locally as pigweed, is probably used by more people than any other weed. In many households, lamb's quarters is the only wild plant ever collected for use in the kitchen and isn't even considered wild by some.

The several varieties got their names from a fancied resemblance to the webbed foot of a goose or a quarter of young mutton, and from the fact that they are sought out by rooting pigs.

Although lamb's quarters found considerable favor with early Indians and was used as much as possible by them through the summer, it was not nearly as abundant as it is today. The advent of large-scale land clearing and roadbuilding allowed it much greater opportunity to expand its range. Today it ranks among the most prevalent of all wild edibles.

The leaves are darker above, lighter beneath.

LAMB'S QUARTERS *(Chenopodium album)*

It speaks well for the native intelligence our forbears possessed in that many of the wild foods they adopted quickly proved to be among the most nutritious foods available. This plant, along with many others, loses a lot after cooking, and if the boiling period is prolonged the values lessen further. Maybe that's just as well, since it might keep us from turning an otherwise delightful side dish into a mass of tasteless, overcooked fibers!

Habitat and distribution: Lamb's quarters prefers drier climates and is especially prevalent in waste ground associated with agricultural development. It flourishes in dry, well-worked soils around gardens, orchards, and farm fields. It is found in suitable areas throughout North America.

Description: The several varieties of lamb's quarters or pigweed are identified by leaves that are roughly triangular, growing on many-branched, upright, fleshy stems. The leaves are deep green above and a grayish-green color beneath that is especially noticeable when the breezes turn the leaves in the sunshine. The leaves are alternate and may be inconspicuously to moderately toothed. The whitish-green center vein is prominent and the surface of the plant usually has a mealy consistency.

In early summer some small green flowers appear near the leaf axils and on the outer limbs. They soon develop tiny dark seeds that grow in short triangular masses, giving the plant a distinctive appearance. The dark seeds appear in fantastic numbers, often over 50,000 per plant!

In the field: The young leaves are excellent in salads, providing a sharp, individual flavor. Boil the leaves—especially the tender leaves and weak stems—as a fresh green that tastes somewhat like cabbage, but is milder.

You can easily collect the seeds in large quantities, grind them, and make a tasty gruel or mush. After this dries (described later), it makes an excellent rough flour to use for making biscuits or hotcakes. A number of Indian tribes used the rough-ground seeds as a cereal for many purposes.

In the kitchen: Beyond the conventional uses as a salad or cooked green, lamb's quarters has almost endless possibilities. Here are just a few different uses.

LAMB'S QUARTERS CANAPES

LARGE LAMB'S QUARTERS LEAVES *20*

PARSLEY *1 tablespoon finely chopped*

,ONIONS *1 cup finely chopped*
RICE *1/2 cup cooked*

DILL *1 tablespoon finely chopped*

ALMONDS *1 tablespoon slivered*
OLIVE OIL *2 tablespoons*

SMOKED PORK SAUSAGE *4 tablespoons*

Wash the leaves and set aside. Mix the remaining ingredients well, until a thick paste results. Put a spoonful of the mixture on the large end of each leaf, roll, and secure with a toothpick. It may require 2 leaves to complete the open-ended roll. Arrange all the rolls in a large skillet and add just enough water to cover the bottom of the pan. (Be careful not to add enough water to allow the rolls to float!) Cook over medium heat. covered, until the leaves are tender, usually about 1-1/2 hours. Add more water whenever necessary to keep the rolls well steamed. These appetizers combine the tangy taste of the leaves with the rich filling and are an excellent addition to a dinner or party. Serves 6 to 8.

BAA-BAA KRAUTKOPF

LAMB'S QUARTERS TOPS
1/2 pound

LINK SAUSAGE *1/2 pound*

ONION *1/2 cup diced*

DRY BREAD CUBES *1 cup*

WHOLE EGG *1, beaten*

TOMATO SAUCE *1/2 cup*

KETCHUP

ONION RINGS

Roughly chop the lamb's quarters top leaves and stem. Mix first 6 ingredients well and pour into a greased loaf pan. Bake in a moderate oven about 1 hour or until the leaves are tender. This meatloaf-type main dish is tangy and delightful. Serve with ketchup, garnished with small onion rings. Serves 6.

Try sprinkling some lamb's quarters seeds over home-baked wheat bread to give it an intriguing flavor of pumpernickel. Or add the seeds to the dough to spread the flavor throughout.

After stone-grinding a substantial number of seeds, boil them into a thick mush. Try a little with fresh berries as a breakfast dish that is filling, nutritious, and very tasty. Spread some of the mush on a flat surface like a cookie sheet and dry thoroughly in the sun or in your oven. This is easily worked into a good flour that makes outstanding dark biscuits from the recipe below—or experiment with it!

HAZEL'S NUTTY BISCUITS

LAMB'S QUARTERS FLOUR
1-1/2 cups

HAZELNUTS (FILBERTS) *1/4 cup ground*

SALT *1 teaspoon*

BAKING POWDER *2 teaspoons*

SHORTENING *4 tablespoons*

MILK *3/4 cup*

BUTTER

Mix the flour, ground nuts, salt, and baking powder. Cut in the shortening with 2 knives or a pastry blender until pea-size or smaller lumps appear. Add the milk and stir briskly until the mixture no longer clings to the mixing bowl. Turn onto a floured board and knead gently about a dozen folds. Roll about 3/4-inch thick and cut the biscuits out. Lightly butter the tops and bake on an ungreased sheet for about 15 minutes. These are surprisingly light and fluffy, with a distinctive nutty flavor. Makes about 12.

LEEK *(Allium tricoccum)*

The wild leek, like the onion, is a member of the lily family and has a distinctive, biting flavor, although not as sweet as the onion. It is closely related to the cultivated leek.

In North America it was a popular and often-used plant among many of the Indian nations, ranging from Florida to western Canada. Early settlers found the leek a fine addition to a venison stew or the basis for a truly wonderful stuffing for wild duck. The journals of Lewis and Clark refer several times to the wild leek as a common ingredient in many of the native dishes they encountered. (One passage in particular referred to a gravy to be poured over roast buffalo. I don't remember the recipe, but the mental picture remains in mouth-watering detail.)

My favorite way of eating wild leeks came about entirely by accident on a fishing trip. I came upon a small patch of leeks while taking a shortcut through the woods to another riffle, so I pulled a half dozen and stuffed them in my vest. For lunch I had brought a roast beef sandwich, but I had put the butter and the mustard on the same slice of bread. Since I really enjoy leeks with a dab of butter, I opened the sandwich and rubbed the cleaned leek on the inside, collecting both butter and mustard. It was incredible! Since then, I always have a spot of mustard on my plate when I eat leeks, and you may want to try that with domestic leeks from your garden.

Habitat and distribution: Wild leeks are found in moist ground and are especially prevalent in the sandy loam along the margins of rivers and streams. They also thrive in the black soils around swampy areas, but usually well above the standing water.

Description: The leek is an annual herb that grows from a slightly enlarged bulb, much smaller than that of the related onion. Two clasping leaves unfurl from the base of the plant. They are broad, pointed, and entire (untoothed). Prominent parallel veins help distinguish the wild leek. The flowers are borne in a terminal umbel, or umbrella-shaped series of short stems. The tiny flowers are pinkish, sometimes nearly white, and ranging to a pale purple. The onion odor is a definite distinguishing characteristic of the leek, which is easily separated from the onions by the broad leaves.

In the field: Gather wild leeks by merely pulling the bulb up from the ground. They seldom grow in soils that make their collection difficult. After the root hairs and outer covering are removed, cook the bulb or eat it raw. It is delicious raw and an excellent addition to soups, stews, and meat sauces. The slightly hot flavor is perfect for adding life to a stuffing for fowl.

In the kitchen: A truly distinguished herb and a favorite in my kitchen. Use the wild leek in place of green onions for a salad. It is especially good as a cooked vegetable.

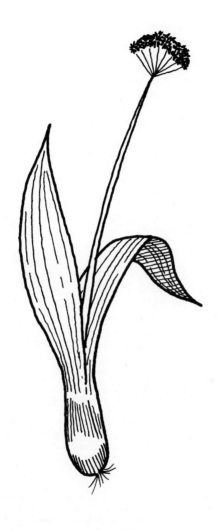

WILD LEEK *(Allium tricoccum)*

STUFFED LEEK HORS D'OEUVRES

LARGE WILD LEEKS *6*
SHRIMP *1/2 cup finely chopped*
CELERY *1/4 cup finely chopped*

OLIVE OIL *1 teaspoon*
LEMON JUICE *1 teaspoon*
PARSLEY *1 tablespoon chopped*

Boil the white portion and about 2 inches of the green part of the leek for just 3 minutes. Drain and chill. After chilling, cut each lengthwise and remove part of the center, leaving 12 boat-shaped leeks ready for stuffing.
TO STUFF: Finely chop the removed center portion of the leeks and thoroughly mix with the remaining ingredients to make a saladlike paste. Carefully stuff the 12 leek halves and chill until ready to serve. Makes 12.

This is a magnificent beginning to a formal wild dinner, setting the stage for the delights that lie ahead!

IRISH FLAG

SMALL WILD LEEKS *6*
BUTTER
CORNED BEEF *1 cup cooked*
WHITE SAUCE *1 cup*

GREEN PEAS *1/2 cup*
BUTTER *1 tablespoon*
SALT *and* PEPPER
PARSLEY

Cut the leeks into 1/2-inch slices and saute in butter. Cube the corned beef into hearty pieces. In a saucepan, combine the white sauce, beef, peas, leeks, and melted butter. Season to taste and simmer for 10 minutes. Garnish with a sprig of parsley. Serves 4 to 6.

GRANDPA'S LEEKY PIE

BASIC PIE PASTRY *1 recipe*
WILD LEEKS *1-1/2 pounds*
BUTTER *3 tablespoons*
SOUR CREAM *1 cup*
DRY SHERRY *1/4 cup*

WHOLE EGGS *3 (separate 1)*
SALT *1/4 teaspoon*
PEPPER *dash*
CELERY SEED *1/4 teaspoon*
CANADIAN BACON *4 ounces*

Line a 9-inch pie tin with dough and set aside. Cut the leeks into thin slices. In a heavy saucepan, saute them until transparent. In a separate saucepan, blend the sour cream, sherry, and eggs (reserve 1 white for use later) along with the salt, pepper, and celery seed; cook over low heat, stirring constantly. When it is thoroughly blended, mix into the sauteed leeks. As this mixture cools, brush the pie crust with the remaining egg white. Pour the leek filling into the crust and cover with the Canadian bacon, sliced very thin. Bake this meat pie at about 300° for 30 minutes or until the bacon is well browned and filling is set. Serves 6 to 8. If you're real hungry, serve with hot whole wheat biscuits or buttered toast. This superb dish can be a main course or served as a complement to a pot roast.

The wild leek is so much superior, in my estimation, to the domestic variety that the foods you cook with it will bear little resemblance. Even though the flavors of the two are similar, the differences are enough to warrant considerable effort to find and collect the wild ones.

AVALANCHE LILY *(Erythronium montanum)*
GLACIER LILY *(Erythronium grandiflorum)*
TIGER LILY *(Lilium parviflorum)*

These plants are included in this guide purely for reference or for use as a survival food. Never pick the three true lilies just to satisfy your own curiosity or as an experiment in wild edibles. In most places they are far too rare to be freely gathered from the wilderness.

They are, however, especially valued as a survival food because of their habitat. As the first two are almost exclusively limited to high elevations, they are quite easy to find for the party delayed by a sudden storm or injured in the high reaches of the mountains. You can eat the bulbs raw or cooked.

My only experience with these plants came when a Forest Service trail crew was forced to reroute a heavily traveled trail in the Cascade Mountains near Mount Adams. The new route went through a good stand of avalanche lily, which necessitated their removal. Except for that particular circumstance, I probably would never have had the chance to eat these

Avalanche lily

Photo by Joy Spurr

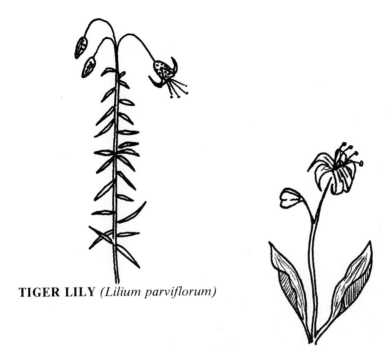

TIGER LILY *(Lilium parviflorum)*

AVALANCHE LILY *(Erythronium montanum)*

GLACIER LILY *(Erythronium grandiflorum)*

outstanding plants, since I feel quite strongly that they should not be gathered for food. (Incidentally, it is to the credit of that maintenance crew that they replanted as many of the lilies as possible on their own time, after the working-day was over. Many of the transplants survived and are still blooming along that stretch of the Pacific Crest Trail in Washington.)

A brief description of each plant is included for identification.

AVALANCHE LILY: A beautiful white lily that grows in the alpine and subalpine meadows of the mountains. The flower is easily identified by the six back-curving petals typical of various members of the lily family. The white blossom has a gold tint deep in the throat. There may be as many as four flowers to a single plant. The avalanche lily is almost the trademark of the high meadow; no other flower looks as much at home in the silent beauty of the high mountains.

GLACIER LILY: Also often called the snow lily, this plant also has the recurved petals that distinguish this family. The brilliant yellow blossom hangs from the graceful drooping stem. The leaves are smooth and dark green. Usually there are two leaves and a single flower. The glacier lily very seldom occurs below 4000 feet. The blossoms appear in the early summer, just a few days after the snows have receded.

Glacier lily

Tiger lily

WILD TIGER LILY: This plant looks almost exactly like the domestic variety. It has several flowers of orange petals with brown or purple spots. The many leaves are scattered around the stem. Some are in whorls, others in alternate poses. If any of these lily plants could be considered a real edible, it is this one, which has a much greater range and distribution than either of the others. It ranges from sea level to the high altitudes, and thus may bloom from early June into late August.

Of the three major lilies discussed here, only the tiger lily has a history of being used by the Indian communities. During the territorial days of the Northwest, a few settlers were recorded as having added it to their diet. It is still quite rare in the wild and probably is considered an endangered species in all of its range. Both the avalanche lily and the glacier lily are classified as rare. It is fortunate that they are legally protected in all of our national parks and forests, which cover nearly all of their habitat.

Please consider these three lovely flowers as just that—lovely flowers—except in the direst of situations. Along with the trillium and the blue camas lily, these plants are much better photographed than digested!

MILKWEED *(Asclepias* species)

There are several species of edible milkweed, but consume them only in reasonable quantities. There are very low levels of toxins in some of the plants, but *Asclepias fascilularis,* distinguished by long thin leaves in whorls on the stem, has particularly high amounts of toxins compared to the other Pacific Northwest species. The two most common forms of milkweed, *A. speciosa* and *A. syriaca,* have been shown to be harmless to humans when eaten in small amounts.

Like many other plants, the milkweed has a curious history as both a food and a medicine. American Indians have long used the young shoots, flowers, pods, and stems as a general food. The medicine men of many tribes prescribed the use of milkweed during pregnancy, in the belief that it would increase the flow of milk in the new mother. It is probable that the popular name is an offshoot of this mistaken belief. (At least, I *think* it's mistaken!) Some authorities attribute the name to the white latex that is found throughout the plant.

Habitat and distribution: The two main species both tend to grow best in dry, open areas, although scattered plants are found in the moister coastal regions. They are not particularly abundant in the damper climate, but are so prolific as to be a pest in some of the interior valleys and plains. They are generally found on wasteland, vacant lots, and along the margins of farm areas, usually in well-drained, dry soil.

Description: The milkweed is a common, fleshy-leafed, one- to two-and-one-half-foot tall plant that may be completely covered with soft hairs or glabrous below. The flowers, which are borne in several dense umbels (that look like umbrellas) on the upper part of the main stem and major branches, are pink to red-purple with conspicuous, incurved, horn-shaped appendages attached just above the reflexed petals. The leaves vary from ovate to oblong and are strikingly veined. A warty pod develops from the ripened ovary on a stout, curved stem. The pod also has a definite curve at the pointed, or outward, end.

In the field: The young shoots and leaves are the best part, becoming very bitter and milky with age. The pod is also edible; collect it before it is fully developed. Cook young stems along with the leaves to add body to the green vegetable. In those areas where the plant is widespread, it is easy to collect a large number of small pods in a reasonably short time. They provide a different and quite interesting dish.

The roots, although reputed to be edible, have never met with wide favor since they contain large quantities of the milky sap and must be practically boiled to death before the bitterness is removed. It is best to simply overlook the root as a source of food.

½" ACROSS

5 PETALS
5 HORNS

White latex flows where a leaf was removed.

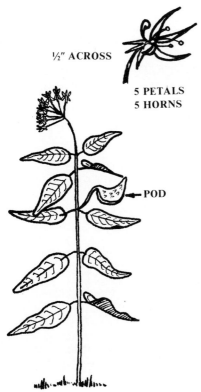

→ POD

MILKWEED *(Asclepias speciosa)*
(color photo, page 167)

The large, pointed leaves of the young milkweed nearly hide the spike of buds at the center.

In the kitchen: Milkweed is a real challenge in the kitchen, especially since the pods are of such a unique shape that they lend themselves to unusual applications. It's a dandy vegetable to play with.

MILKWEED POD SOUP

MILKWEED PODS *1/2 pound*
MILKWEED SHOOTS *1 cup*
SALT
BUTTER
ONION *1/2 cup*
coarsely chopped

MUSHROOMS *1/2 cup sliced*
BEEF STOCK *4 cups*
WHOLE EGGS *2 hard-boiled,*
whites only
HAM *1/2 cup cooked and cubed*
SALT *and* PEPPER

Boil the pods and shoots together in salted water for about 10 minutes. Drain and slice into 1/2-inch pieces. In a soup kettle, melt a dab of butter and lightly saute the onions and mushrooms. Add the stock, the coarsely chopped egg whites, and the remaining ingredients, including the milkweed parts. Season to taste and simmer for 20 minutes. You'll find that the flavors of both the beef and ham are recognizable in the milkweed parts. This is a hearty, chunky soup that makes a fine rainy-day luncheon. Serves 8.

THREE-LEGGED MILKWEED

LARGE BERMUDA ONION 2
LARGE CELERY STALKS 4
MILKWEED PODS 1/2 pound
sliced
MILKWEED LEAVES 1/2 cup
chopped
FLOUR 3 tablespoons

CHICKEN STOCK 1 cup
MUSHROOMS 1/4 cup sliced
SALT and PEPPER
CHERRY TOMATOES 4,
quartered
ALMONDS
SOY SAUCE

Cut the onions into eighths and the celery into 1/4-inch strips. Boil them with the milkweed parts until the onion is semitransparent; drain and set aside. In a large saucepan, blend the flour into the chicken stock to thicken slightly. Put the boiled vegetables and mushrooms in, cover, and simmer over low heat for 15 minutes. Season with salt and pepper, add the cherry tomatoes and simmer for 5 more minutes. Garnish with slivered almonds and serve with soy sauce alongside. This great chickeny vegetable dish is reminiscent of Chow Yuk and is a simple, delightful main course for a meatless dinner. Serves 6.

MILKWEED SEAHORSES

MILKWEED PODS 12
MILKWEED LEAVES 1 cup
chopped
CRABMEAT 6-1/2-ounce can
ONION 1/4 cup chopped
TOMATO PASTE 3 tablespoons

CELERY 1/4 cup chopped fine
BUTTER 1 tablespoon
CHEDDAR CHEESE 6 thin slices
LEMON WEDGES
STUFFED OLIVES (optional)

Boil the pods and leaves separately for 5 minutes. Drain both and set aside. Combine the crabmeat, onion, tomato paste, and celery. Cut the pods along one side and stuff with the crabmeat mixture. On a heatproof dish, arrange the stuffed pods over a bed of the cooked greens. Dot the pods with butter and lay the cheese over them. Put under the broiler only long enough to melt the cheese over the pods and onto the greens. Serve with lemon wedges. Each pod may be decorated with a thin slice of stuffed olive to represent the horse's eye. This is a colorful and delightful dish. Serves 6.

CREAMWEED

MILKWEED LEAVES and
STEMS 2 cups chopped
WHITE SAUCE 1-1/2 cups
PEARL ONIONS 1/2 cup

PEPPERONI SAUSAGE
1/2 cup chopped
PARSLEY

Boil the milkweed parts, drain, and add the white sauce immediately. Over low heat, stir in the pearl onions and pepperoni sausage pieces. Cover and simmer until the onions are semitransparent. Garnish with parsley. Serves 6.

MINER'S LETTUCE *(Montia perfoliata)*
SIBERIAN MINER'S LETTUCE *(Montia sibirica)*

These two closely related plants are probably the finest salad greens among all the wild edibles and are at least as good as the domestic varieties in a fresh green salad.

It would be impossible to find out how far back this delicate little plant has been used as food, but the very earliest records of native life in North America indicate it was popular. Early explorers in western Canada found the natives using miner's lettuce in the simplest of all possible ways: they sat down in a thick patch and pulled the leaves and stems around them, contentedly chomping away until they had eaten their fill. The exploring party laughed at the natives for "grazing like a dairy-cow," and went back to camp to treat their own scurvy. White settlers quickly recognized the value and fine flavor of miner's lettuce and used it frequently.

The Siberian form was first discovered in Siberia (obviously) and is still used in the lower reaches of that cold land as a popular salad green. It apparently grows as far north as the timberline. I have found *M. sibirica* growing in large patches throughout the southern half of Alaska, where it was a historic native food.

In the Siberian miner's lettuce the larger upper leaves may appear almost to be a single leaf.

TINY 5-PETALED FLOWER NOTICEABLY NOTCHED WITH RED LINE ON PETAL

MINER'S LETTUCE *(Montia perfoliata)*

SIBERIAN MINER'S LETTUCE *(Montia sibirica)*

Miner's lettuce leaves form a shallow cup with the stem protruding from the center.

Habitat and distribution: One or the other of these two plants is found almost everywhere except the arid and desert sections of the continent. Both flourish in moist ground, especially near or under coniferous trees. In areas where broadleaf trees are scattered through a second-growth forest, they can grow as thickly as grass, making collection pretty simple. Miner's lettuce is delicate and is almost never found growing without the protective shade of larger trees.

Description: Miner's lettuce is a fleshy annual or perennial plant that generally grows from a slender taproot. There are several large-stemmed leaves around the base and usually only a single leaf or pair on the middle of the stem. The key to identifying miner's lettuce is the stem apparently growing through the middle of two opposite leaves which are usually joined to form flat disks. From the disk rises a raceme of small white flowers. Siberian miner's lettuce is best identified by the five-petaled flower with a deep notch in each petal and a single red line running the length of each petal. The stems are prominently reddish, while the dark green leaves are glossy and have tiny distinct veins.

In the field: This is a simple plant to collect. You can eat the stems and leaves raw or boiled like any other leafy green. Their flavor is similar to chard, but much more delicate. Pull the tiny roots up by the handful and cut into a suitable container with knife or scissors. Even though they are slow to collect, they are really delicious when lightly boiled. They have a crisp flavor that compares with water chestnut. If you boil the leaves and stems, be sure not to overcook these delicious greens. Drop them in boiling water for just three or four minutes before serving.

In the kitchen: Both are a flavorful addition to salads.

CHILLED SIBERIAN SALAD

MINER'S LETTUCE *about 1 quart*

TUNA *6-1/2-ounce can, drained*

ONION *2 tablespoons chopped*

GREEN PEPPER *1 tablespoon chopped*

THOUSAND ISLAND *or* FRENCH DRESSING *or* LEMON

Mix the ingredients well, so the tuna, onion, and pepper are well scattered throughout. Sprinkle lightly with cold water and refrigerate until ready to serve. Dress with Thousand Island or French dressing, or with lemon. Serves 6 to 8.

APPALACHIAN CAESAR

MINER'S LETTUCE *about 1 quart*
CATTAIL SHOOT *1/2 cup sliced*
DRY BREAD *1/2 cup cubed*
SARDINES *2, chopped*

ONION RINGS *1/2 cup*
OLIVE OIL *2 tablespoons*
DRY MUSTARD *dash*
WORCESTERSHIRE SAUCE *dash*

Toss all the ingredients well, so the pieces are evenly coated with the olive oil. Serve without dressing. This is the simplest of salads and makes use of very inexpensive ingredients. Expand it into a quite formal salad by the addition of a tablespoon of wine vinegar, a teaspoon of lemon juice, 1 raw egg, and a springling of Parmesan cheese. Toss vigorously and serve. Serves 6.

SUNBURNED MINER

MINER'S LETTUCE LEAVES, STEMS, *and* ROOTS

CHEDDAR CHEESE *1/2 cup finely grated*

RADISHES
LEMON WEDGES

Boil the miner's lettuce parts for just 3 minutes. Drain and place on a heatproof dish. Sprinkle the cheese over. Broil in the oven until the cheese has thoroughly melted into the greens. Garnish with a sliced radish and lemon wedge. The roots add a nutlike flavor and crispness to this fine dish. Serves 6.

WILD MINT *(Mentha* species)

There are several species of mint found in suitable habitats. Of these, two—wild peppermint *(Mentha piperita)* and wild spearmint *(M. spicata)*—have been introduced from the Old World and have become well established after escaping from cultivation. The native species include Canada mint *(M. canadensis)* and field or brook mint *(M. arvensis).*

The earliest recorded use of wild mint on this continent was as a medicine. The dried leaves were burned in ceremonial fires by some medicine men, pervading the atmosphere of the long house with the sweet, pungent aroma. A tea that was steeped from the leaves was used to cure fever, while another tea that was brewed from specially selected fresh leaves was purported to be helpful in preparing for a vision or communicating with the spirits. The Indian beliefs in mint as a medicine have at least some basis in fact, for wild mint is used today in the production of commercial medicines.

Except as flavoring, wild mint is not a popular potherb because of a bitterness in the leaves and an overwhelming flavor. The Indians apparently felt the same way, for there is little evidence of mint being used as a cooked vegetable. However, it was quite often favored for adding taste to otherwise bland foods.

Typical of all mints, Canada mint has leaves in opposite pairs, each pair being almost exactly 90 degrees rotated from the leaves immediately above and below.

MINT *(Mentha arvensis)*

Peppermint

Spearmint: notice the unusual leaf structure.

Canada mint. The stem is square.

One of the really beautiful aspects of wild mint is the fragrance that hangs along a cool stream bank in spring and summer. After you walk through a thick stand, crushing leaves underfoot, the sweet aroma begins to waft along with the breezes. Often when I am fishing along some small stream, I pause for lunch amidst a patch of wild mint. As I lie back to let my sandwich digest, that fragrance, perhaps more than any other, is indelibly etched on my memory. In the heat of summer, the refreshing mint odor seems to cool the air even more than the stream.

Habitat and distribution: Wild mint is found in wet ground, generally associated with rivers, streams, ponds, and swamps, and even along the margins of large lakes. It grows in such places throughout the continent. A hardy plant, the mint is even found in the saline soils near the ocean.

Description: The mints have two prominent features besides the distinctive odor. First, the stem is square. The leaves are in opposite pairs, each pair being almost exactly 90 degrees rotated from the leaves immediately above or below. The leaves are toothed to entire, and small clusters of blossoms grow at the numerous junctions between leaf and stem. In the Canada mint, the stems are a dark purple, but they are green in spearmint and peppermint.

The tiny flowers may be white or pink but are more often a soft purple. The flower appears to have four petals, which constitute the four lobes of the corolla, the upper one being considerably larger than the other three—another distinguishing characteristic. Stems and leaves are often hairy. These mints, the true mints, are not typical of the larger mint family, *Lebiatae:*

In the field: The mints are not only easy to find but are a real joy to collect. The air around you and even your hands and clothes soon smell of mint. Simply pluck the stems off near their base. In some recipes, the six or eight leaves that grow from a single stalk are sufficient. The terminal four leaves are in an attractive sprig and make an excellent garnish. You can dry the leaves for tea or use them fresh. Green leaves are better for flavoring salads or cooked dishes, but dried ones are much finer for tea.

I particularly enjoy adding a few shredded leaves to a salad. In the bush, when a dressing isn't available, use it to offset the sourness of sheep sorrel and the bitterness of dandelion leaves.

In the kitchen: Since wild mint is not used as the main ingredient in any dish, it is not entirely honest to list a group of recipes here that include mint as a flavoring. In most cases the recipe works quite well with the mint omitted. Instead, you will find wild mint listed in several other recipes throughout this book. But here are two in which the mint is essential.

ABOMINABLE JELLY

HIMALAYA BLACKBERRIES *1 gallon*
WILD MINT LEAVES *1 cup*
APPLE *1, pared and cored*
SUGAR *about 8 cups*

Mash the blackberries in a large kettle along with the mint leaves and the apple. Boil until all are soft. Strain off the juice and put the mass of cooked berries in a clean white cloth. Drain the berry pulp until you've gotten every drop of juice out. Carefully measure the juice, then bring it to a rolling boil and add 1-1/2 times more sugar than you had juice. Pour in jelly jars and seal with melted paraffin.

This clear sweet jelly will make those winter morning breakfasts sparkle with the fresh taste of mint and the remembrance of a springtime past. The apple, incidentally, is optional. Sometimes it helps the jelly to set, and it really doesn't change the flavor enough to notice. Makes about 6 pints.

CLASSIC MINT JULEP

ICE
WILD MINT *1 plant*
SUGAR SYRUP *2 teaspoons*
BITTERS *dash*
BOURBON WHISKEY *1-1/2 ounces*
POWDERED SUGAR

In a tall glass of crushed ice, place the leaves from your mint, reserving the top sprig for decoration. Pour over it the sugar syrup and bitters and stir briskly with a stirring-spoon or muddler, being sure to bruise the mint leaves and release their flavor. Pour in 1 ounce of bourbon and stir well to chill the glass. Add ice to within 1/2-inch of the top and add the remaining bourbon. Again, stir briskly until the glass becomes frosty. Dampen the mint sprig, dip it in powdered sugar, and garnish the drink with the sprig and two long straws. Makes 1 drink.

This drink became famous for combatting the heat of a muggy summer evening in a most hospitable manner—a fame it justly deserves!

MUSTARD *(Brassica* species)
BLACK MUSTARD, TANSY MUSTARD, YELLOW MUSTARD

SEED PODS
½ TO 2 INCHES

MUSTARD *(Brassica nigra)*

The several members of the mustard family discussed here all have yellow flowers, small curving seed pods, and leaves that have a pronounced basal lobe. The mustard plants are another group that was a bit difficult to find in the early days but has really flourished following the advent of large-scale cultivation. Mustard now ranks among the more numerous common weeds.

Mustard apparently met with mixed reactions from the diversified Indian tribes, being quite popular among some and looked upon with disdain by others. Because of its unique flavor, it seems to elicit the same kind of response today.

If the mustard plants were at all universal in use among the native communities, it was medicinally. The seeds were dried and prepared into mustard plasters that were reputed to cure anything from colds and chilblain to weak-mindedness and gastric disorders. An old book of home remedies on my shelf reports the use of mustard as an infallible cure for dyspepsia and constipation, but it was also quite helpful in treating poisoning and worms. Mixed with water and applied to the outside of the body, it is supposed to purge any manner of ills. I don't doubt it a bit! As hot as mustard seed can be, it probably took away the skin along with the complaint! From an infinitely more practical point of view, mustard greens were very popular among some tribes, and a number of long-standing favorite dishes included this zesty green in their preparation.

This tall, slim mustard is typical of the ones that grow in wetter areas. The leaves are smaller. The flowers are just beginning to open.

This mustard plant shows the deeply lobed leaves near the base of the plant.

The mustard family is widely represented in the world of cultivated plants, including cabbage, cauliflower, Brussels sprouts, kale, turnip, rutabaga, broccoli, and of course, mustard. The wild mustard that you find will probably be one of two very abundant weeds, *Brassica nigra* or *B. juniea,* although the lesser-known types are handled in exactly the same ways

Habitat and distribution: Mustard is found in waste ground, fence lines, ditches, and fields. The only limitations appear to be high elevations and desert sections, even though the plant is found in very arid, semidesert regions in the extreme Southwest. It is plentiful throughout mòst of the continent.

Description: Mustard is a thick, branched annual or perennial that usually reaches four feet in height. The familiar flowers are tiny, yellow, and borne in long, vertical racemes at the top. The seeds are spherical and arranged in one row or two or more distinct rows in each locule (see drawing and photos of this unusual structure). The leaves are generally deeply lobed near the base of the plant, becoming moderately lobed at midpoint and nearly entire at the top. The lower half of the stem may be stiffly hairy.

In the field: The leaves of all the members are safe and tasty. Simply pluck them from the stems. The lower leaves are larger and tougher but retain about the same flavor as the younger upper leaves. A few authorities maintain that you can eat the young leaves raw, but they may be both tough and strongly flavored. Shred a few in your next wild salad. The pungent, almost peppery flavor can be a true asset to an otherwise bland salad, especially if you are in the field and forgot to bring along the oil and vinegar!

Collect the seeds and use as a flavoring, lightly sprinkled over a salad. Large numbers of the seeds may cause some gastric discomfort, so use them sparingly. Any cases of poisoning on record seem to indicate that the seeds, particularly immature ones, were the culprit. Mustard has been included on lists of plants poisonous to livestock but is not listed as dangerous to humans, which seems to indicate that large quantities are necessary to be at all harmful.

The flowers are also edible, but I calculate it would take an hour or more per mouthful to collect them.

The leaves of this variety have wide lobes near the base. Another mustard plant showing the unusual leaf structure.

All true mustards have this odd arrangement of seed pods.

In the kitchen: Because of a fine, individual flavor, I prefer the greens just boiled for five minutes and served with butter and lemon juice, but there are many fine recipes that include mustard greens as major ingredients. I found this recipe for prepared mustard in an 1895 cookbook, and it is the tastiest and smoothest you'll ever put on a sandwich.

"OLD YALLER"

MUSTARD SEED *2 tablespoons finely ground*
SUGAR *1 teaspoon*
SALT *1/2 teaspoon*

CAYENNE PEPPER *dash*
CREAM *1 tablespoon*
BUTTER *1 tablespoon*
VINEGAR *(optional)*

Mix the first 4 ingredients in a heavy cup (stone preferred) and put over very low heat. Pour in a little boiling water and stir constantly until the mixture thickens. Take off the heat and stir in the butter and cream. One tablespoon of vinegar may be added if desired. The butter and cream make this preparation much smoother and richer than any you can buy! Makes enough for 6 sandwiches.

SKINNY MUSTARD STEW

HAM BONE
MUSTARD GREENS *1 cup chopped*
POTATOES *1-1/2 cups diced*

WHOLE KERNEL CORN *1/2 cup*
ONION *1/4 cup diced*
SALT *and* PEPPER

In a large soup pot, put the ham bone and just enough water to cover. Boil vigorously for 15 minutes. Reduce the heat and add the greens, potatoes, and corn. Simmer for 30 minutes, then add the onions and season to taste. Another 15 minutes over low heat and it is ready to serve. Simple and delicious, with a fine mixture of well-defined flavors. Serves 6.

STINGING NETTLE *(Urtica dioica)*

The stinging nettle is one of the best-known plants. If you are ever in doubt of its identity, a quick swipe with the back of your hand will quickly remove it. The red welt will remain for several hours to confirm your suspicions! It seems a bit incongruous that you can safely eat this delicate devil that protects itself so efficiently.

The Indians have long used the stinging nettle as a green vegetable, but the idea didn't really catch on with the settlers, who apparently preferred to pick a plant less likely to bite back. Perhaps the recipes were a little much, as well: I read one recently for a nettle stew that included half a cup of red ants and a dozen minnows, complete with heads, entrails, and eyeballs. It probably was pretty tasty, but I guess if that were my introduction to stinging nettles, I never would have tasted them! (Fact is, I *still* haven't been able to get those ants to sit still long enough to find out if I can collect half a cup!)

Stinging nettle

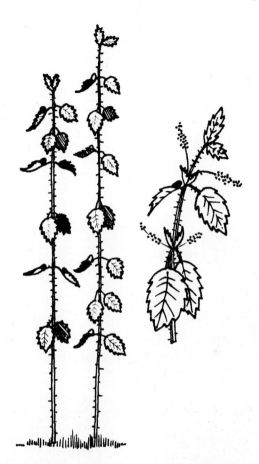

Nevertheless, the nettle became an important part of the diet in a number of villages. It was most commonly a green vegetable simply boiled and eaten, but often the shoots were laboriously collected and eaten raw.

Nettle stings are usually relieved by rubbing them with any combination of leaves from three different nearby weeds. Even though that remedy sounds straight out of the oldest of home remedy books, it seems to work, I suppose because of a combination of factors found in the other plants. At any rate, it works for me.

Blue camas (page 45)

Devil's club *(page 83)*

Oregon fairy bells (page 255)

Labrador tea *(page 127)*

Note the short, bristly hairs on the stalks and leaves.

Habitat and distribution: Stinging nettles require quite a bit of moisture and are found along stream banks, swamps, and other wet soils. They are found along river courses and shaded areas in even the drier sections, but they cannot survive in direct sunlight on open ground in the semiarid regions.

Description: The stinging nettle is a tall plant with a definitely ribbed stem that is sometimes almost square. The leaves are opposite, deeply veined, and evenly toothed. The stalk, petioles, and leaves are covered with short bristly hairs that are hollow and deliver the stinging oils when touched.

Small flowers, usually greenish but sometimes becoming a light purple, are borne in vertical racemes near the top. The main identification character is the hair that provides the sting.

In the field: As might be expected, it is best to collect this plant with a pair of gloves. After you have had considerable experience with stinging nettle, you'll find you can safely handle them bare-handed, but it takes some doing. I find that if I grasp the plant quickly and firmly, I can hold either the heavy stalk or the leaves without being stung. It is only when you brush the plant lightly or accidentally that you are stung. However, it would take far too long to gather a sufficient number for a meal without the gloves.

The young leaves, stems, and tops are by far the best for cooking, and they need to boil for only two or three minutes to be tender and tasty. Most people cook them too long in order to be sure they are safe from the stings, but about 15 seconds in boiling water renders them harmless. If the leaves are particularly large or old, it may take boiling in two waters to remove the bitterness of age.

Pick the young, tender, pink shoots just as they appear, or even before by removing the moss around the base of a cluster of nettles. You can eat them raw or cooked and they are an excellent potherb. They are sweet, crisp, and a fine addition to the wilderness salad. Normally, the shoots are found for only a few days each spring, so the leaves are the major edible portion.

In the kitchen: Nettle is a tasty, delicate plant that is easily ruined by too much cooking, so most recipes provide for boiling very briefly. This limits its use, but here are a couple of ways to make the leaves tender, keep the beautiful emerald green color, and maintain the delicate flavor. Despite its fearsome reputation, the stinging nettle could become one of your favorite wild edibles.

STINGI-NEDDLE SOUP

NETTLE LEAVES *1/2 pound*   BROWN RICE *2 cups cooked*
CHICKEN STOCK *5 cups*   SOY SAUCE *1/2 teaspoon*

Wearing rubber gloves, rinse the leaves and wad them into a tight mass. Slice the mass of nettles into 1/2-inch widths and plunge into boiling water. After 1 minute, remove from heat and rinse in cold water. Set aside. In a large saucepan, bring the stock to a boil. Add the rice and soy sauce and reduce the heat. As soon as the stock stops boiling, add the nettles. After 1 minute, remove from the heat and serve. This filling and delicious soup perfectly preserves the young nettle's flavor. Serves 6 to 8.

NETTLE GREEN-AND-GOLD

NETTLE LEAVES *1 quart*   LEMON JUICE *1 teaspoon*
BACON SLICES *2, fried crisp*   WHOLE EGGS *2, hard-boiled*

With rubber gloves, wash the leaves in cold water and let drain. Bring a pot of fresh water to a boil. Plunge the leaves into the water and immediately crumble the bacon in with them. Let boil for about 3 minutes, then pour into a colander to drain while very hot. Do not rinse. Put the greens in their serving dish, sprinkle with lemon juice, and arrange slices of egg over the dish. Serve as a side dish to fish or fowl. The brilliant green color and fresh flavor will complement the light meats perfectly. Serves 4.

Hazelnut (page 257)

Dogwood (page 250)

Fireweed (page 115)

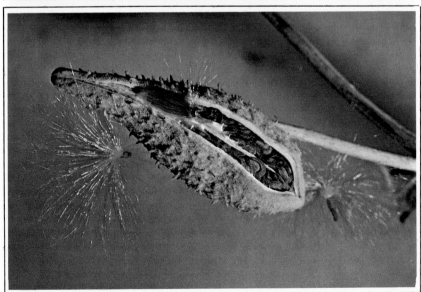

Milkweed pod (page 142)

WILD ONION *(Allium* species)
CLUSTER LILY *(Brodiaea* species)
WILD HYACINTH

These two large groups of plants, representing about 100 different species, are handled here as one, since they have about the same appearance when not blooming and can be used in exactly the same ways. The *Allium* branch of the family is better for long-term storage. All of these, and the cultivated onion as well, belong to the lily family. The *Allium* species include the cultivated white and yellow onions, Welsh onions, leeks, green onions, and chives. Obviously, they are related by taste as well as botanical similarities.

Even though the wild onions and *Brodiaea* were long used by the Indians in North America, they were not usually used in the manner that we have become accustomed to. Instead, the natives commonly roasted large numbers of them in the coals of a fire until they had formed a brown, sticky mass. They were quite sweet after such preparation and were eagerly devoured in large quantities.

This method produces a superb dish, but I find that it also produces heartburn of monumental proportions, even when taken in moderation. When one thinks of the results of a large feed in a pre-antacid society, assuming the digestive system was about the same as mine, the picture is comic, indeed!

The wild onion's colorful history included dozens of medicinal uses, both in Indian cultures and in the folk habits of the European immigrants. In combination with garlic (another *Allium* relative) it could cure just about anything—or at least so the practitioners of the earlier days preached. Looking over a few of the old wives' home remedies, it seems onion was better at preventing illness than curing it. It was seriously considered the best way to ward off cold, consumption, headaches, and bad teeth. When Columbus first visited Hispaniola, every native hut had a cluster of onions hanging over the door to ward off the evil voodoo spirits. As recently as the mid-1800s superstitious slaves in the American south believed garlic was essential to keep werewolves at bay.

Fortunately for us, the onion had a parallel history as an important food and delightful flavoring. Hardly a kitchen in the country today is without a shaker of onion salt, and American housewives purchase millions of pounds from the supermarkets annually. It is probably as familiar as any other food we eat, yet we hardly think of it as a staple. Rather, we think of it as a condiment or something to make a sandwich a little better. Among the wild foods, I like to use it as a major item.

Some detailed studies have found little compositional differences in *Allium* and *Brodiaea,* so I've taken the liberty of lumping them together under

WILD ONION *(Allium* species*)*

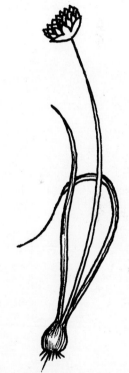

CLUSTER LILY *(Brodiaea* species)

Beargrass *(page 31)*

Scotch broom *(page 189)*

Wild rose *(page 284)*

Rosehips (page 284)

"onion." I'm sure that both the chemical and taxonomic communities will suffer simultaneous coronaries, but we country types still understand each other!

Habitat and distribution: The 65 or so *Allium* species generally prefer moist soil and rather shady locations, although there are a few exceptions. The *Brodiaea* species, numbering over 30, are usually found in drier, open ground. The combination means that almost everyone can find one or the other in virtually any region.

Description: Wild onions are herbaceous plants with thick basal leaves growing from an underground bulb, which may vary in size according to the species. The leaves are smooth, always basal, and usually narrow, but broad in a few cases. The leaves often number only two. A central stem develops on which the flowers and seeds will be borne. The *Allium* species usually have a large number of tiny flowers in a flat umbel, while the *Brodiaea* generally have several large blossoms. Check the drawing to determine the differences. The various plants have a tough covering over the bulb that varies in pattern, but all have many nearly transparent layers inside the cover. All the *Allium* species have a definite onion odor, but it may be absent from some of the *Brodiaeas*.

In the field: You can usually collect the bulbs of the wild onions in the same manner as the onions in your garden—grasp the plant and pull straight up. In late summer, if the ground has become firm, a little digging may be required.

Use only the bulb and white portions of the stem and eat them raw or cooked. Always discard the leaves and upper green. The green portions have been known to absorb pollutants from the air and selenium from the soils and are considered unsafe. The bulbs are virtually always safe, if eaten in normal amounts. Even cultivated plants, if eaten in large quantities, have been known to cause poisoning.

The small onion bulbs are a superb addition to a salad and are especially flavorful when roasted in the coals of a campfire. A handful of small onion bulbs boiled with a pot of lamb's quarters is an excellent camp dish.

In the kitchen: The value of the wild onion in the kitchen cannot be overestimated. I imagine at least half the recipes in this book call for onion, and the wild variety is usually preferable to the domestic. I doubt that I'd be able to cook without onions.

ONION OMELET SUPREME

MILK *2 tablespoons*
DRY WHITE WINE
1 tablespoon
WILD ONIONS *1/2 cup*
chopped
SALT *and* PEPPER
WHOLE EGGS *2, beaten*
OIL

SMOKED FISH *2 ounces,*
flaked
MUSHROOMS *1/4 cup sliced*
SWISS CHEESE *1/4 cup*
grated
LETTUCE
TOMATOES

Beat the milk, wine, onions, and seasoning in with the eggs. Pour into a lightly greased skillet. DON'T STIR OR TURN! Allow to fry for about 4 minutes, or until the edges are firm. Place the smoked fish in the center of the omelet, put the mushrooms in a thin layer over the fish, and top that with a layer of cheese. Carefully fold the edges over the center, making sure the inner layers are covered. When the bottom is golden brown, carefully turn the omelet over and remove from the heat. Serve this fantastic dish on a bed of lettuce, garnished with fresh slices of tomato. With fruit and toast it is one of the finest breakfasts I've ever eaten. Serves 2.

ONION JUE-BILLEE

BEEF STOCK *1/2 cup*
SOY SAUCE *1 teaspoon*
WATER CHESTNUT *1/2 cup*
sliced
CHERRY TOMATOES *4, halved*

WHOLE WILD ONIONS *1 cup*
POD PEAS *1 cup*
MUSHROOMS *1/2 cup sliced*
CELERY HEARTS *1/2 cup*
sliced

Put the stock and soy sauce in a heavy skillet over medium heat. Pour in all the ingredients, cover tightly, and simmer until the onions and pods are tender. Place the vegetables in a serving dish and pour the remaining stock over before serving. A fantastic meatless main dish! Serves 6 to 8.

BEEFY ONION STEW

POTATOES *1-1/2 cups*
cut in 1-inch cubes
STEW BEEF *1 pound*
CARROTS *1/2 cup diced large*

WHOLE WILD ONIONS *1 cup*
CELERY *1/2 cup,*
rough-chopped
SALT *and* PEPPER

In a heavy stewpot, put a layer of potatoes. Add all the meat as a second layer, put a layer of carrots on top, then add the onions in a fourth layer. Finally, add a layer of celery. Put in enough water to cover the top layer, sprinkle salt and pepper on top of the water, and cover. Cook over moderate heat so the stew does not boil vigorously, but cooks thoroughly. When the celery has cooked on top, each of the succeeding layers will be perfectly done. Don't stir this stew until just before serving. Serves 8.

Squaw currant (page 247)

Kinnikinnick (page 264)

Blue elderberry (page 253)

Golden currant (page 247)

Serviceberry (page 290)

Salal (page 287)

Salmonberry (page 289)

PEPPERROOT *(Dentaria* species)
TOOTHWORT, DENTARIA

The common name pepperroot comes from the sharp, mustardlike flavor of the root, which is pleasant and zesty, despite the sharpness. Another common name, toothwort, is derived from the many scales resembling teeth that are found on the roots of some individuals.

Even though pepperroot is found in abundance in many areas, very little is known about this plant or about its history. We know that dozens of Indian tribes used it, but neither the recipes nor the popularity of the plant has been recorded in the material I have read. More was written in colonial America and later than earlier in our history.

The plant is unobtrusive and often overlooked in the wild. I have had little experience with it and have never tried cooking it. It has apparently always been eaten raw. It has a fine flavor reminiscent of watercress, but is much more substantial.

Habitat and distribution: Pepperroot is found in the coastal and mountain areas, with some species occurring in the eastern United States and Canada as well. One, the mountain dentaria *(D. macrocarpa),* is apparently limited to the shady woods on the east slopes of the Cascade Mountains in Oregon and Washington, extending into southern British Columbia.

Description: Pepperroots are perennials growing from tuberous rootstocks which are edible. The rootstock is usually covered by scales or "teeth," although at least one species has an elongated, horizontal rootstock that is scaly and crinkled. The erect stems are about a foot high with a few leaves, palmately cleft or compound near the stem tips. A few basal leaves appear that generally differ from those above. The leaves may be widely variable, even within a species. The flowers are borne in a sparse raceme and are usually rose to purple, occasionally white. They invariably have four petals in a cruciform or cross arrangement.

In the field: Pull or dig the thick, fleshy rootstock; pare and eat it raw. It has a rather zesty, pleasant flavor. I can find no historical reference to the plant's being cooked and would experiment cautiously. Be content with the unusual flavor of the raw rootstock.

In the kitchen: The rootstock should be a fine addition to a salad and would probably make an excellent relish, although I have no recipes.

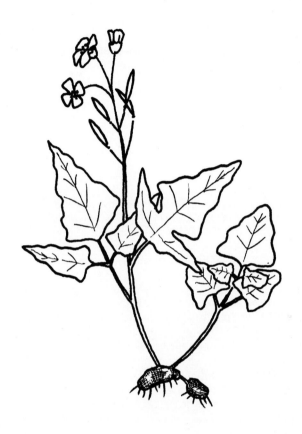

PEPPERROOT *(Dentaria pulcherrima)*

PIGWEED *(Amaranthus* species)

Here's another widely known weed that has done much better since the beginning of cultivation but has not been widely recognized as an edible.

Some confusion exists over the name, since "pigweed" is shared by several common plants, including lamb's quarters. In a way, the same name for these two plants is justified, since both have excellent flavors and are quite nutritious. The similarity between pigweed and lamb's quarters continues into the use of their seeds, which are excellent for baking, making mush, and flavoring other foods.

One species of *Amaranthus* can impart a pink coloring to other foods without substantially changing their flavor and thus found wide use among the early Indians in ceremonial foods. While most of the normal dyes were either poisonous or unpleasant tasting, *Amaranthus* gave them a chance to color special ceremonial foods.

Although the leaves of the couple of dozen species were an important part of the diet of many tribes, the seeds were more valuable as a source of gruel and flour. They were easily ground, cooked with water, and dried. The resultant flour made a light dough that probably was used in making the forerunner of today's meat pies. A favorite dish of some southwestern Indians was fresh meat wrapped in a dough of pigweed flour and baked—delicious! The seeds were also popular with corn meal and meat, formed into cakes, and cooked. This dish was used until very recently by some outlying tribes and may still be today.

The ability of pigweed to absorb minerals from the soil may be a drawback in some cases. If found in or adjacent to fields where nitrogen fertilizer is used, collect the plant only in small quantities, since the buildup of nitrates might be quite high. It is advisable to collect them well away from places where such fertilizers are applied, although in normal quantities they would still be safe.

Habitat and distribution: Pigweed is found almost anywhere, in soils ranging from rich to thin and in climates from moist to very dry. It apparently is excluded only from alpine and desert sections.

Description: Pigweed is an annual herb with a many-branched stalk. The leaves are alternate at regular intervals and are generally entire. They are linear ovate in shape, or occasionally pointed. The flowers and seeds grow from smaller stems that appear in the leaf axils. Several species have a gritty feel when the leaves are rubbed between the fingers.

In the field: Gather the leaves as any other leafy green. They are excellent when lightly boiled; cook them as soon after picking as possible to preserve their flavor. They have been compared to asparagus in flavor, but remind me of very young spinach leaves, although more delicate.

PIGWEED *(Amaranthus retroflexus)*

It is easy to collect the mature seeds from the plant, where they grow in remarkable numbers. Eat them whole or grind between two stones to make a gruel or mush. You can then dry the mush and powder to make a fine flour. The addition of a little water and fat, or a bit of milk if it is available, will produce a superior hotcake for breakfast.

In the kitchen: This excellent plant is best cooked and served alone for the fine flavor. You may use the lamb's quarters recipes, or try this one if you have a quantity of ripe seeds. They provide a unique flavor.

PIGGY-PIGGY PATTIES

PIGWEED SEEDS *1 cup*
CORNMEAL *1/2 cup*
PORK SAUSAGE *1 pound*
WHOLE EGG *1*

BUNS
LETTUCE
TOMATO
ONION

In a large mixing bowl, combine first 4 ingredients well. Form into thick patties. Broil, without seasoning, until the patties are thoroughly done. Serve on soft buns with lettuce, tomato, and sliced onions. Serves 6 to 8.

PERFECT PIGWEED

PEARL ONIONS *1/2 cup*
SALT *1/4 teaspoon*
HAM *or* BEEF *1/2 cup cooked*

PIGWEED LEAVES *2 cups*
LEMON WEDGES

Boil the onions in salted water for about 5 minutes. Add the cooked meat and pigweed and boil for an additional 5 minutes. Serve with lemon wedges. Serves 6.

This is a fine way to use a small amount of leftover meat. I once added a little leftover venison heart, and the result was outstanding.

PIGWEED SPICE SALAD

PIGWEED LEAVES *1 cup*
chopped fine
MARINATED GARBANZO
BEANS* *or*
SALAD-BEAN COMBINATION

ONION *1/2 cup chopped*
GREEN PEPPER *1/4 cup*
chopped

Boil the pigweed leaves for 5 minutes. Rinse in cold water and leave in strainer or collander until well drained; chill. Pour the garbanzo beans or salad-bean combination, including the vinegar marinade, into a salad bowl. Stir in the pigweed, onion, and pepper. Chill until time to serve. Drain off most of the vinegar and toss well. A refreshing and delicious summer luncheon salad. Serves 8.

*Commercially packed, including spiced vinegar.

PLANTAIN *(Plantago* species*)*

BROAD-LEAVED PLANTAIN *(Plantago major)*

NARROW-LEAVED PLANTAIN *(Plantago lanceolata)*

In the narrow-leaved plantain the leaves do not have a definite petiole.

More than 20 species of plantain abound throughout North America, and they are collectively perhaps the most widely distributed of all the wild edible plants, with the exception of dandelion. Even so, most people don't recognize these weeds until they are pointed out.

The species fall into two major groups: broad-leaved and narrow-leaved. They can be eaten and handled identically.

The plantains were regularly used as food in the native communities throughout America and were equally familiar to the early European and Asian. Even today several are cultivated in parts of the Orient. (Don't confuse them with the cooking banana, also popularly named plantain.) The plantains, still occasionally called "Indian wheat," provided an excellent source of flour to the early Indians.

Habitat and distribution: Plantain seems to be absent only from the high mountains, deserts, and deep forests. Elsewhere it grows in profusion. The best place to begin looking is in your garden and lawn, where it often flourishes.

Description: The various plantains are identified by their parallel-veined leaves growing in a basal cluster from the roots. In the broad-leaved species the petioled leaves are broadly elliptical. The narrow leaves range from grasslike to quite broad, but they have no definite petiole. The accompanying photos and drawings make the distinction clear.

The seeds of the broad-leaved plantains are borne on thick spires, clustering in a conical spike near the top. In the narrow-leaved species, the seeds are in a stout spike atop a spindly stalk. The stalk is also clearly veined or ribbed.

In the field: The broad-leaved species are far superior in flavor and edibility. The narrow-leaved plants tend to be somewhat bitter and tough. The quality of the leaves varies greatly according to growing conditions. I have collected some that were a fine delicate leaf ideal for a spring salad. At other

The broad-leaved species have petioled leaves.

Pluck the leaves of broad-leaved plantain near the top of the tougher stem.

times I have cooked them for a few minutes and found them roughly comparable to a square of green felt! Generally, the broad-leaved plantain is best in spring, but you can find new leaves throughout the summer with a little looking. The young leaves make a particularly fine cooked green, tasting much like a young spinach leaf. If you use the narrow-leaved species, they are best cooked in a sweet water, with sugar or honey added. In salads, combine them with berries or sweet leaves to counteract any bitterness.

The broad-leaved plantain seeds, dried and stone-ground, produce an excellent flour, ideal for breads and flapjacks. To the ground flour, add a little milk, fat, and salt, and cook on a hot griddle. With a handful of huckleberries mixed in, it makes a great camp breakfast.

In the kitchen: Use the leaf in many of the same ways as similar plants. Refer to the sections on dock or sheep sorrel for additional recipes.

DANDY PLANTAIN SALAD

PLANTAIN LEAVES *1-1/2 cups*
DANDELION LEAVES *1-1/2 cups*
ONION *3 tablespoons chopped*
CROUTONS *1/2 cup*
TURKEY *1/2 cup chopped*

WHOLE EGG *1, hard-boiled*
MINT SPRIGS
LEMON WEDGES
SALAD DRESSING

Wash the leaves; mix well with the onion. Toss the croutons into the salad lightly. Sprinkle the chopped turkey over the top and arrange thin slices of hard-boiled egg over all. Garnish with mint sprigs and wedges of fresh lemon. Dress with your favorite salad dressing. Serves 6.

PLAIN PLANTAIN

PLANTAIN LEAVES *3 cups*
WILD HONEY *2 tablespoons*

Boil the leaves for about 5 minutes. Drain all but about 1/2-inch of the water and add the honey. Cover and simmer until the leaves are tender. An excellent way to prepare the tender leaf. Serves 4 to 6.

NARROW NOODLE CASSEROLE

SUGAR *3 tablespoons*
WATER *2 cups*
NARROW-LEAVED PLANTAIN
2 cups
EGG NOODLES *1 cup*

ONION *1/4 cup chopped*
CHICKEN *1 cup boned*
SALT *and* PEPPER
MILK *1/2 cup*

Dissolve the sugar in 2 cups of water. Soak the raw plantain leaves for 30 minutes. Drain and wash. Boil the leaves with the noodles until both are tender. Drain, mix with the onion and chicken, and put in a casserole. Season to taste and pour the milk over. Bake covered in a moderate oven for about 30 minutes. This casserole is a bit juicy but has an excellent flavor that will become a favorite. Serves 6.

PLANTATION PLANTAIN

PLANTAIN LEAVES *3 cups*
BACON STRIPS *4*

ONION *2 tablespoons sliced*
SWISS CHEESE *1/2 cup grated*

This outstanding dish takes 3 steps—boiling, frying, and broiling. Boil the leaves until tender and fry the bacon until it is just transparent. Arrange the leaves in a heatproof dish, pour the bacon fat over them, and put the onion slices over all. Sprinkle with a layer of the grated cheese. Cut the bacon strips into squares and arrange them over the cheese. Broil until the bacon has thoroughly browned and the cheese has melted over the onion and plantain. This rich, somewhat salty dish is great with a baked fish or roast. Serves 6.

RICEROOT *(Fritillaria lanceolata)*
CHOCOLATE LILY

This intriguing plant is widespread in the Northwest. A close relative, *Fritillaria kamtchatcensis,* ranges into Canada. They are similar and are used in the same manner.

Undoubtedly, many Indian groups used this plant for food, but little record is found of such use and little is known of it. It is included in only a couple of current books about the plants west of the Rockies. The name chocolate lily is a bit misleading, since this plant has no chocolate characteristic and is not a lily. It probably comes from the mottled brown flower that appears in late spring. The name riceroot fits it much better, since the large bulb is covered with many small nodules that look much like rice grains.

When a friend introduced me to this special plant as a small boy, I was surprised to find it tasted a bit like raw potatoes—the kernels looked like white bugs feeding off the central bulb. He rubbed a few of the kernels off and ate them, urging me to do the same. After trying them they became one of my all-time favorites.

Although I am a bit mystified that this plant has not appeared before in any of the popular volumes on wild edibles, I'm certainly not unhappy; it gives me the opportunity to introduce it to you, and it has kept collecting pressure fairly low. Even though it is a beautiful flower, I have found it abundant enough to collect without any pangs of conscience.

Habitat and distribution: The riceroot is found mostly in the Northwest and prefers moister ground in the normally dry pine forests. It is found in deep woods and along swampy ponds and stream banks. Its relative *F. kamtchatcensis* is found in the wetter climates west of the Cascade Mountains from Oregon to British Columbia.

Description: Riceroot is a slender, erect perennial with whorls of thin, narrow leaves. They may occur as whorls of from three to six leaves, occasionally only two, at the common axil. The drooping flowers are brown, lightly mottled with green, composed of six petals. The petals do not curve back as is common with real lily blossoms. The key to identification is the large central bulb surrounded by the tiny white nodules, like grains of rice, that give it the common name.

In the field: These lovely plants are abundant along many of the Northwest's finest trout streams and are a great complement to freshly fried trout. The entire bulb is edible. It probably could be eaten raw with impunity, but I advise cooking. The flavor is improved and its safety is guaranteed. Boil the bulbs and serve with butter or gravy or refry them with meat.

Riceroot bulb surrounded by tiny white nodules.

RICEROOT *(Fritillaria lanceolata)*

Riceroot

In the kitchen: Riceroot has a fine flavor and is a fun plant to work with. The methods of cooking it seem to be endless, and all the recipes I have tried have worked out better than I had any right to expect. You can use them for any application that calls for either rice or potatoes, as well as invent a few ways of your own. I will just include a single spectacular recipe.

RICEROOT a la RUSS

RICEROOT *3 cups*
BUTTER *3 tablespoons*
ONION *1/2 cup chopped*
CELERY *1/2 cup chopped*

MUSHROOMS *(optional)*
LEFTOVER PORK *1 cup chopped fine*
SOY SAUCE *2 teaspoons*

Boil the riceroot until it just begins to soften. Drain and set aside. In a large skillet, saute the onion and celery in butter until transparent (the addition of a few sliced mushrooms at this stage doesn't hurt a bit). Stir in the cooked riceroot and pork. Keep turning the mixture as you would fried rice until the riceroot begins to brown in the butter. Add the soy sauce, stir in well, cover, and lower the heat. Turn the riceroot occasionally until quite soft. This filling and delightful dish has a flavor that simply cannot be described. It is probably the wild dish that I like better than any other. Serves 6.

SCOTCH BROOM *(Cytisus scoparius)*

(color photo, page 171)

Scotch broom

This widespread nuisance has overtaken so much land in the western coastal states and British Columbia that it's hard to believe it was introduced recently. A native of Europe, Scotch broom was planted in the vicinity of Victoria on Vancouver Island by an English settler who was apparently homesick for a glimpse of the old sod. He must certainly have gotten that glimpse, and a lot more. Within a few years Scotch broom had gained a foothold on the island and had blown onto the mainland near Point Roberts. Fifty years later this weed had reached California. Today, thousands of dollars are spent every year trying to eradicate Scotch broom from cultivated fields. In many places the fight has simply been given up.

It is no less amazing that someone has found at least a minimal use for this plant as a wild edible. I admire his ingenuity.

Habitat and distribution: Scotch broom has become established in climates from very wet to very dry and virtually all kinds of soil conditions, but so far it is limited to the three coastal states and western British Columbia. That could easily change in years ahead, since this tough shrub seems to adapt to any condition and spreads rapidly.

Description: Scotch broom is a highly-branched evergreen shrub that reaches a height of about 10 feet under ideal conditions. Usually it is shoulder high and grows in immense thickets, covering many acres. The tiny needlelike leaves are sparse on the dark green stems, and the main stalks are greenish-gray. Bright yellow flowers cover the plant in the springtime, causing many people severe allergic reactions. The flowers are pealike and about an inch long. The flowers give way to masses of hanging green pods, fringed with a definite hairy covering, particularly along the margins. The pods become blue-black upon ripening.

In the field: Grind the roasted ripe seeds as a coffee substitute. They are safe used this way and make a rather good replacement. DO NOT EAT the fresh buds and pods, since they contain the same alkaloidal toxins as the green foliage of the bush.

In the kitchen: I once tasted a remarkably good homemade dill relish made of Scotch broom. Try pickling the young pods; they are then safe, unusual, and delicious. The pickling process is simple, but must be followed carefully:

Soak the young pods in a heavy brine of vinegar and salt. They must be held under the brine for about 24 hours. To accomplish this, make a large wooden grid, place over the floating mass, and weight it with stones. It is unsafe to use a metal screen or metal weights for this purpose, since the acids in the vinegar may react with the metals, adding a poison to the brine that the pods would absorb. Following the 24-hour soaking in this brine, rinse the pods carefully in cold water and put them in any good pickling solution. I prefer a garlic and dill pickle solution that gives them a fine, sour taste not unlike kosher pickles. They should again be weighted and left until they will not float of their own accord. After this, they are suitable for use and can be sealed and stored like any good pickle.

I've included no other recipes since it is highly unlikely that you would use the plant in any manner other than pickled and it probably won't be your favorite coffee substitute. The young stems, incidentally, after hours of cooking closely resemble a handful of galvanized nails, but are probably a little less flavorful!

SHEEP SORREL *(Rumex acetosella)*

Several species of this plant abound, but they are easily identified as close relatives to the dock plants by the unusual seed structure. They are as variable in use as the common docks and are similar in food values.

Because of a fine flavor, considerable bulk, and easy availability, it was popular among the early native settlers. (Don't confuse sheep sorrel with wood sorrel, listed elsewhere in this volume; they are not related.)

Sheep sorrel is often called Indian tobacco because of the hundreds of tiny brown seeds that cling to the upper stalks. When stripped off, they do look like a tobacco but are entirely unsuited to the purpose. I have no record of the seeds being used as a food.

Habitat and distribution: Sheep sorrel is found in various soils and climates. It often seems to prefer dry ground and waste areas, but is equally found along the edges of forests and near the margins of cultivated fields.

Description: Sheep sorrel is an erect, branched annual distinguished by basal leaves with a distinct triangular shape. Small clusters of flowers are borne on terminal racemes and soon give way to groups of squarish brown seeds. The upright stalk and leafy stems are often tinged with red.

In the field: Sheep sorrel is an excellent spring green but is seldom used as a raw vegetable. The leaves are particularly flavorful when collected in the spring, but the older leaves are also quite flavorful if you boil them sufficiently to make them tender. This causes some vitamin loss, but most of the vitamin A will remain in the plant. The leaves are known to contain small quantities of oxalic acid, but not in quantities large enough to be harmful. Even though cooking does not reduce the content of this acid, it is safe to eat the leaves in small quantities. It is probably unlikely that anyone could physically eat enough to cause any serious discomfort.

The young leaves and stems are best when lightly boiled in salted water and served with a dab of butter or lemon juice. They are especially fine when a little ham or bacon is added during the boiling.

Sheep sorrel leaves.

SHEEP SORREL *(Rumex acetosella)*

The seeds of sheep sorrel cling to the upper stalks.

In the kitchen: You can use sheep sorrel in many ways at home.

SMILEY'S SORREL SOUP

SHEEP SORREL *1 cup chopped*   THIN BEEF STOCK *3 cups*
CAULIFLOWER *1 cup in small spears*   ONION *1/4 cup chopped*
STEW BEEF *1/2 cup small chunks*   WHOLE KERNEL CORN *1/2 cup*

Put all ingredients in a large soup kettle. Bring to a boil and lower heat. Simmer for about 30 minutes, until the sorrel and cauliflower are tender. The stock will thicken slightly during cooking, making a hearty soup that is especially good on a cold afternoon. Serves 6 to 8.

SWEET, SWEET SORREL

SHEEP SORREL *3 cups*   MUSHROOMS *1/2 cup sliced*
SALT *1/4 teaspoon*   LEMON WEDGES
HONEY *3 tablespoons*

Soak the sorrel leaves for 30 minutes in salted water. Drain, but don't rinse. In fresh water, put the honey, sorrel, and mushrooms. Boil rapidly about 5 minutes, drain, and serve. Garnish with lemon wedges. The honey imparts a unique, delicious flavor to the sorrel. Serves 4.

SKUNK CABBAGE *(Lysichitum americanum)*

Here is another common plant that makes one wonder how anyone ever found out it was edible. If any plant is a candidate for pure oblivion this one is, but it is actually reasonably good after cooking. I doubt that I would ever place it on my list of favorites, but others are worse.

Skunk cabbage has a long but spotty record as a wild edible in North America, generally finding its widest use during years when other food was scarce. It was never a staple of the Indian diet and was not adopted by the white settlers.

Skunk cabbage contains calcium oxalate, which must be removed by boiling and discarding the water before the plant is edible. In this respect it parallels taro, a near relative in the Pacific islands, which also requires extended cooking to become edible.

Habitat and distribution: Skunk cabbage is associated with wet, swampy ground. Generally a low-elevation plant, it is sometimes found in surprisingly high locations, especially in Idaho and Montana. It ranges as far north as Alaska and down into California.

Description: Skunk cabbage is typified by its large, basal, oblong leaves, heavily veined. The main central vein has a triangular cross-section and is well defined along the back of the leaf. The root is quite large and fleshy. A thick seed spire is partially enclosed by a rounded, yellow, bractlike leaf. A key to identifying this plant is the odor—the stems and leaves smell unmistakably of skunk!

In the field: You can roast the starchy rootstalk very well and pound it into a white flour. Or cook the rootstalk into a thick mush, dry, and then pound between stones to make flour.

Eat the young leaves after several boilings, after which they become almost white and quite soft and taste somewhat like an overdone domestic cabbage. You *must* cook this plant very well in several changes of water to remove the calcium oxalate. Otherwise, you will experience a burning sensation, and your lips and tongue can actually be injured. It is best to try a tiny sample to make sure you have cooked it long enough. The same is true of the roots.

Skunk cabbage

Look for the curled yellow sheath near the center of the skunk cabbage, which protects the knobby seed spike.

In the kitchen: I'll pass along one simple recipe. You might like to try skunk cabbage in other ways, but the preliminary boiling should always be complete.

LI'L STINKER DINNER

SKUNK CABBAGE STALKS *and* LEAVES *2 pounds*

CORNED BEEF BRISKET *about 3 pounds*

MEDIUM ONIONS *12*

SALT *and* PEPPER

DRY MUSTARD *1/4 teaspoon (optional)*

PARSLEY

HORSERADISH *and* MUSTARD MIXTURE

Boil the skunk cabbage, cut into 2-inch widths, through at least 5 boilings, completely changing the water after each. Continue to boil until a small sample indicates a bland, soft cabbage flavor with no burning sensation. Drain and set aside. In a large pot, cover the brisket with just enough water to keep it all boiling. Cook at a low boil for 2 hours. Add the onion and seasoning to the water and continue to boil for 15 minutes. Add the preboiled skunk cabbage and cook for another 15 minutes. You may wish to lower the heat and add 1/4 teaspoon of dry mustard to the water and simmer for a few minutes before serving. Garnish with chopped parsley and serve with a tangy horseradish and mustard mixture. Serves 8.

This dish depends on how efficiently you boiled the cabbage to remove the calcium oxalate, which is why you sample it before committing the expensive beef brisket. If sufficiently precooked, it imparts a rather bland but interesting flavor to the stew.

THISTLE *(Cirsium* species)

There are over 30 species of thistle, virtually every region being the home of a half dozen or more. Most common are Canadian thistle, elk thistle, Indian thistle, and bull thistle. The identification of any species is largely academic, since all are used in much the same manner, although there is some difference in flavor.

The history of the thistle as food is as colorful as any of the wild edibles, being responsible for the survival of a good many pioneers and explorers. Lewis and Clark were forced to turn to thistle at one point on their westward trek from the headwaters of the Mississippi. Many years later Truman Everts wrote of using thistle to survive while he was lost in the area that is now Yellowstone Park.

An old Indian legend tells of a powerful chief who was cast into a wasteland where only the lowly thistle could grow. The chief dug up the roots of the thistles and survived. The Great Spirit, rejoicing that a favorite son had endured, placed the thistle throughout the lands, so that any brave who was lost or injured could have food at hand in any season.

A young bull thistle.

THISTLE *(Cirsium vulgare)*

Habitat and distribution: True to the terms of the legend, some kind of thistle grows practically everywhere from the subarctic to the deserts of Mexico. It is found in virtually every habitat, ranging from below sea level to alpine slopes. It varies from sparse to abundant. Some species flourish in dry, open land, while others prosper in wetter situations. Almost anyone can find a thistle nearby at any time of year.

Description: Thistles are leafy, upright annuals or perennials. They are often woolly with armed bracts surrounding the flowers. The leaves are almost invariably alternate, sessile, and heavily armed with sharp spines. The flowers are usually purple or red, but may occasionally be yellow or white. Cottony seed heads appear after the flowers in late summer.

In the field: Although identification is not difficult for thistles in general, it may be somewhat hard to distinguish one species from another. Handle all the same way—carefully. The sharp spines can be quite uncomfortable. Every species provides edible roots and stems.

The roots are the major food item, although the stems are also tasty as a cooked green. Wash and peel the roots, then roast or boil. You may occasionally have to boil older roots in two waters to remove bitterness. They

Thistle has a thin carrotlike root.

One kind of thistle showing the characteristic sharp spines on the leaves.

are a trifle bland, but are good when cooked in a soup or a stew. Young roots are tasty when lightly boiled, then sliced into rounds and fried in fat. They tend to brown nicely, providing something of the appearance of country-fried potatoes. I particularly like them along with fresh pan-size trout.

You can also boil the roots into a thick mush that can be eaten as is or dried into a weak flour. It is best mixed with water and fat and cooked into a flat cake that is filling, but a little tasteless.

Boil the young stems as a green, but take great care to peel them completely. Tiny spines can grow from the skin and take some of the fun out of eating them. The skins also contain most of the bitterness of the stems, and removal produces a much more palatable dish.

In the kitchen: In combination with other foods, the thistle is a table treat.

THISTLE DEW NICELEE

THISTLE ROOT *3 cups pared and sliced*

FLOUR *2 tablespoons*

BUTTER *1/4 cup*

PEPPERONI SAUSAGE *2 ounces*

MILK *1-1/2 cups*

SALT *1 teaspoon*

DRY MUSTARD *or* PARSLEY FLAKES *(optional)*

PARSLEY SPRIGS

Boil the thistle until almost tender. Drain and let stand in colander 15 minutes until fairly dry. Dredge with the flour and dot with butter in 3 layers in a baking dish, alternating with paper-thin slices of the sausage. Heat the milk and dissolve the salt in it. Pour it over the thistle and sausage mixture. Bake in a moderate oven about an hour. Dry mustard or parsley flakes are optional seasoning to suit your own taste. Garnish with parsley sprigs and serve with a pot roast—a great way to treat an unwanted weed! Serves 6.

THISTLEDOWN CAKES

THISTLE ROOT *2 cups pared*

FLOUR *1 cup*

SALT *1 teaspoon*

WHOLE EGGS *2*

ONION *1 tablespoon grated*

OIL

APPLESAUCE *1 cup*

This one takes a bit of time but is well worth it. Boil the thistle roots in water to cover until they are a thick mush, usually about 2 hours. Drain well, then spread on a cookie sheet to dry completely. In the sun this takes several hours, in a low oven about 2 hours. When completely dry, put them in a sturdy mixing bowl and work them with a wooden spoon until only a dry, white powder appears. This is thistle flour. Add to it the other flour and salt. Beat in the eggs and add just enough water to make a thick batter. Stir in the onion. Fry the cakes in a hot skillet with just enough fat to keep from sticking. When the cakes are done on one side, turn and continue to cook until they are crisp. Put a large spoonful of applesauce on each while it is still hot. Makes 12 to 16 cakes.

Serve with scrambled egg and country sausage. If the thistle flour is prepared the day before, this is a wonderful breakfast dish.

THISTLE AU CHEN

BEEF STOCK *1-1/2 cups*

GREEN PEPPER *1/2 cup sliced*

SMALL CARROTS *6*

LARGE THISTLE STALKS *6*

MUSHROOMS *1/2 cup sliced*

GREEN ONIONS *6*

SALT *and* PEPPER

Put the beef stock in a heavy skillet. Add all the vegetables, season, and simmer, covered, until they are very tender. (Cut them into pieces about 1 inch long before cooking, if desired.) This simple combination dish provides 6 distinct flavors in a potpourri that is unusual and practically foolproof. Serves 6 to 8.

TRILLIUM *(Trillium ovatum)*

   This is the familiar "Easter lily" or wake robin, depending on where you live. It is one of the earliest of all wild plants to flower, ushering in the spring season.

Trillium   *Photo by Joy Spurr*

Commit trillium to memory as a possible survival food but never collect it for the fun of it. It is quite palatable, but its beauty and relative scarcity dictate that it should not become part of a menu simply because it is available. It is included solely for information, and I discourage anyone from picking it.

Habitat and distribution: This delicate plant is found in deep woods and moist forest areas. It is especially common west of the Cascades in Oregon, Washington, and British Columbia but occasionally has been found in the Rocky Mountains and northern California.

Description: Trillium is a low perennial with a characteristic whorl of three leaves at the top. The single flower is white, pink, or purple with three petals over three prominent leaflike bracts.

In the field: Except for survival, this plant is best observed and left alone. If essential, boil the three upper leaves. The roots are not edible, being a powerful emetic.

In the kitchen: Remember trillium from outings the previous spring. That's all!

WATERCRESS *(Nasturtium officinale)*

Common old watercress probably would not normally be thought of as a wild edible, there being a good supply in the local markets from time to time. It is, nevertheless, abundant and widespread.

Our historical records of this interesting member of the mustard clan go back probably as far as any plant in the wild inventory. We know of some use of watercress as much as 5000 years ago, and it very likely was used well before that.

Perhaps the most interesting of the dozens of medical uses attributed to it was in Roman times. It was prescribed as a cure for those who were insane or possessed by devils. When Pliny recorded man's medical knowledge in about 62 A.D., he listed over three dozen uses for watercress. Among these was using smoke of the burning plant to drive away snakes. A few whiffs of fresh watercress were supposed to counteract the venoms of reptiles, scorpions, and spiders.

The Greek physicians of that same period had quite different feelings about watercress. Although they felt it was a pretty good aphrodisiac, they thought it would harm the child conceived under its effect. (Pliny, meanwhile maintained it had a dulling effect on the erotic senses.) The Greeks wrote that watercress would harm the stomach but at the same time would rid the system of worms. Fortunately, not many people could read in those days, and the plant continued to be a favorite for salads and cooked greens.

More recently, watercress was a popular salad and addition to sandwiches in Great Britain, and the American Indians were eating this delicious plant when the Pilgrims arrived.

Although its use medicinally is questionable, it has good food value.

I think you will like the fresh, delicate flavor of the wild watercress, even when compared to the varieties available at the local supermarket. Here is a good example of the difference between a freshly collected plant and one that has languished in the greengrocer's bins for who-knows-how-long!

Habitat and distribution: Watercress is found in slow-moving streams and brooks but does not do well in small ponds, stagnant water, or very cold lakes. It grows throughout the continent.

Description: Watercress is an aquatic plant that may be floating, erect, or prostrate, usually in large masses. The roots are firmly anchored, with white nodules sometimes showing at the base of the fleshy stalks. The compound leaves are pinnate, lightly veined, and entire. Tiny white flowers appear in terminal racemes. Seed pods are carried upright, as with most other mustards.

In the field: You can gather watercress easily in large bunches from the edges of the streams in which it grows. Be careful to collect it only from unpolluted water, since the foliage may absorb harmful compounds. Eat the leaves raw in a salad or as an excellent cooked green. They have a trace of the tangy flavor of other mustard plants.

Watercress

In the kitchen: Although watercress is almost always served as a salad green, it provides an excellent, unusual flavor after boiling as a vegetable.

CLASSIC CRESS SALAD

CHERRY TOMATOES *6*
GREEN ONIONS *6*
SHARP CHEESE *1/4 cup grated*
WATERCRESS *1 cup*

WOOD SORREL *1 cup*
CROUTONS *1/2 cup*
FRENCH *or* THOUSAND ISLAND DRESSING

Slice the tomatoes and onions into small pieces and toss all ingredients together. Serve with a French or creamy Thousand Island dressing. The sharp taste of the watercress is complemented by the slightly sour flavor of wood sorrel and the sweeter dressing. Serves 4.

CRACKLING CRESS

WATERCRESS *2 cups*
MUSHROOMS *1/2 cup sliced*
ONION *1/4 cup chopped*

DRY WHITE WINE *1/4 cup*
LEMON WEDGES

Boil the watercress and mushrooms in water to cover for about 5 minutes. Lower the heat and add the onion and wine. Simmer for about 15 minutes or until leaves are very tender. Garnish with lemon wedge. An outstanding side dish to a baked or roasted fish. Serves 6.

KELLY'S CREAMY CRESS

CREAM SAUCE *2 cups*
BLUE CAMAS LILY BULBS *12*

WATERCRESS *1-1/2 cups*
ALMONDS *1 tablespoon sliced*

Make your favorite cream sauce. Simmer the camas and watercress in the sauce until the bulbs are soft and slightly transparent. Keep the heat low so the sauce does not boil or thicken appreciably. Just before serving, stir in the almonds for crunchiness and added flavor. Serves 6.

WATER PLANTAIN *(Alisma* species)

WATER PLANTAIN *(Alisma plantago-aquatica)*

The water plantains, although not related to the other plantains, have a certain similarity in leaf structure but differ in habitat and use.

There is some confusion concerning the technical grouping of these plants. Some authorities list only one or two species, while others list more than three. It is probably true that *Alisma geyeri* and *A. triviale* are the more widespread, but *A. plantago-aquatica* is certainly more familiar to me. The differences are relatively unimportant for our purposes. All are similar and are eaten in the same manner. They vary from the common plantains in that the roots are eaten instead of the leaves.

There is little historical record of this plant being used in any parts of this country by early settlers or natives, yet an occasional reference in some obscure writings leads me to believe it was used in at least a few places. I found one case of the plant's being used for some time and then abandoned by coastal Indians on the Olympic Peninsula in Washington. This particular species grew in boggy meadows in the foothills of the Olympic Mountains, but the Indians did not range up there very often during the growing season. I have found the plant in that locale in fairly significant concentrations.

Habitat and distribution: Water plantain is found in almost any aquatic or swampy circumstance, but it is quite scarce west of the Cascade range except for a few isolated spots in the Olympic Mountains. It is much more prevalent in the pine forest of the interior sections.

Description: Water plantain is an upright perennial with several glossy green basal leaves that have parallel veins. They may grow up to eight inches long. The fleshy, bulbous rootstock supports several leaves, but generally only one flowering stalk, which may reach about three feet. The white flowers are very tiny. The seeds are borne on the flowering umbels and are almost rectangular and ribbed.

In the field: It is reasonably difficult to collect in any large numbers and is a trifle complicated to work with. I'll limit discussion to field uses, since I have not had an opportunity to cook it in the kitchen. Dry the white, bulbous roots thoroughly before cooking. The strong flavor is lessened somewhat by the drying process, but remains rather overpowering. Boiling in several waters also reduces the strength of the flavor. They somewhat resemble potatoes in flavor after considerable cooking, but their pervading flavor remains, which I don't much care for—but maybe you'll enjoy it.

Eat the plant in limited quantities until you determine whether it will cause you any gastric discomfort. Although I had no ill effects, a companion complained of a mild upset stomach. Whether the water plantain was the culprit cannot be established, but it might be advisable to take a few precautions.

WOOD SORREL *(Oxalis oregana)*

Wood sorrel, often known as sourgrass, is among the most common of all plants growing under the heavy canopy of our coniferous forests. Virtually everyone who has ever wandered away from the roads has seen this pale green cloverleaf. Surprisingly enough, there are more than 10 species of wood sorrel, but the differences are minute.

The history of wood sorrel is involved and colorful. From the northern reaches of Europe to the coastal valleys of Oregon, it has long been used by natives of a dozen countries and backgrounds. This delicate little plant has been found in sauerkraut, sweet pies, salads, and stewpots of a thousand villages and a hundred different tongues. That it is no longer used to any extent is a testimony to the poor judgment of a developing civilization. As a child, I ate sourgrass whenever I went walking in the outdoors and enjoyed it immensely (and I still do!). A friend once brought me a jar of homemade kraut containing wood sorrel, which I greatly preferred to the typical cabbage concoction. The mother of an old school chum once gave us a "green rhubarb" pie that we found was made of wood sorrel, and it, too, was outstanding. I guess the finest product I ever tasted from wood sorrel was a white wine made by an old gentleman near Rabbit Creek, Alaska. It was puckering-dry, delightfully flavorful, and rivaled a fine imported Chablis in bouquet and heady taste. (I never learned the recipe, an oversight I have regretted to this day!)

Although a lot is known about the history and usage of wood sorrel, it has been surrounded by a lot of half-truths and misconceptions. One old tale that *is* true, however, is that overeating wood sorrel can cause severe gastric problems. The plant contains varying amounts of oxalic acid, which gives it the characteristic taste. When it is made into a kraut or pie, it is quite possible to get too much, and your stomach will make you regret your overindulgence. It is doubtful that anyone would eat enough to prove serious, but a "green apple stomachache" could easily result. Using it in salads or as cooked greens, it would be nearly impossible to overdose yourself on sourgrass.

Habitat and distribution: Wood sorrel is found in shady, moist habitats on all continents. It ranges from the wooded highlands of the Southwest far into Canada and Alaska and is found in suitable places throughout the continent.

Description: There is little trouble identifying this dainty plant in the United States. The slender stems are quite fleshy, supporting compound leaves which have three leaflets. The pale green leaflets each have a definite center vein and are deeply notched at the outer margin. The tiny five-petaled flowers may be white, pink, yellow, lilac, or rose. The leaves are the key to identification, being unique in the deeply notched cloverlike trifoliolate leaflets.

In the field: You can easily collect the leaves from the thick patches of wood sorrel that often carpet the forest floor. They are excellent raw in a salad or can be cooked as a substitute for spinach. By adding a bit of sugar to a cup of cooked leaves, you can make a rough pie filling to bake in the reflector oven of your campfire. Eat them in limited quantites until you get used to them.

Tiny blossoms hide among the pale cloverlike leaves of wood sorrel.

In the kitchen: Although a great many different dishes are made from wood sorrel, I'll limit recipes here to several best uses.

SOURGRASS SAUERKRAUT PROCESS

WOOD SORREL   SALT

Collect lots of wood sorrel. Wash carefully, shake off all the excess water, and weigh the leaves. For each pound of leaves, you need 2 teaspoons of salt.

Slice the damp leaves and stems into thin portions and thoroughly mix in the salt. Pack the mass tightly into a stone crock to within a couple of inches of the top. (If you don't have a crock, use a heavy plastic bag inside a metal container. If the bag ruptures, discard the whole mixture because of the possibility of contamination from the metal. Placing the bag in a gallon glass jar is considerably safer!)

Cover the crock with a clean cloth and put a weighted cover on top so the natural brine will rise to the top, wetting the cloth. (Close the top of a plastic container with a clothespin.)

Check the crock daily. When fermentation begins, skim off the foamy scum each day, wash the cloth and cover, and replace. Continue until fermentation stops. (The same is required of the plastic-bag method, but no cloth or cover is required.)

The kraut can then be preserved by heating to about 180°, putting into jars with a little of the brine, and sealing tightly.

NOTE: You may have to add a little water during the packing of the pickling crock, but only a scant amount. If the kraut turns tan or brown, too much of the natural liquid has been fermented out. You'll have to discard the batch and start again. Make sure the finished kraut is well sealed in canning cars or it will spoil during storage.

This is one of the tastiest krauts you'll ever make. Anyone familiar with the methods for making regular sauerkraut will not have trouble with wood sorrel.

SPRING SORROW SALAD

WOOD SORREL LEAVES *1 cup*   SMALL WILD ONIONS *4*
MINT LEAVES *about 12*   RED HUCKLEBERRIES *1/2 cup*
CATTAIL SHOOTS *1/4 cup chopped*   SALT *and* PEPPER
MINER'S LETTUCE LEAVES *1 cup*   LEMON WEDGES

You can collect these 6 wild edibles in the same general area at the same season. Mix well, salt and pepper the top of the salad, and serve with a wedge of lemon. A refreshing, spring treat! Serves 6.

SOURGRASS SALAL SUPREME

WOOD SORREL LEAVES *2 cups*   HAZELNUTS *1/4 cup sliced*
FIRM SALAL BERRIES *1/2 cup*   SALT *and* PEPPER

Boil the ingredients together in just enough water to cover. Season to taste, drain well, and quickly rinse in a colander before serving. Don't overcook this dish, as the mealy berries will discolor. The slight sweetness of the berries combines well with the tartness of the leaves, while the nuts add a full body to the dish. Serves 4.

YELLOW WATER LILY *(Nuphar polysepalum)*

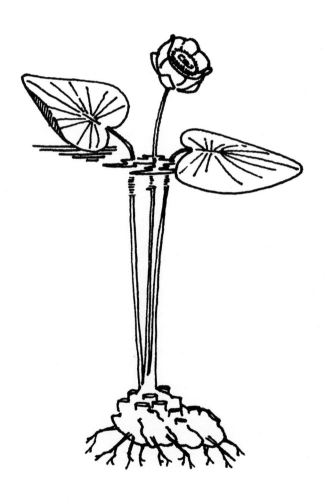

There are two things that strike awe in the person who first collects this common aquatic plant: first, the incredible size and shape of the rootstock, and then the remarkably different ways it is used as a food. From the rather complacent look of the leaves and flower, you would never guess that a giant rootstock lurks in the mud below. Sometimes the rootstock weighs 20 pounds or more.

In many early native cultures, the yellow water lily (more correctly, the yellow pond lily) was an important staple, providing flour, starchy vegetables, an interesting confection, and a widely used green vegetable.

This large aquatic plant also figured in the travels of Lewis and Clark, being purchased from Indians at several different places in their journeys. Although it did not become famous for its flavor, the water lily nonetheless provided considerable food during some of the leaner portions of the trip. They found the Klamath Indians gathering the seeds for a dish called "woka" which resembled popcorn in both flavor and appearance. Since the movies had not yet been invented, popcorn was not as widely known as it is today, and the explorers were properly impressed.

Habitat and distribution: Yellow water lily is found in freshwater ponds, shallow lakes, and slow-moving streams. It ranges from Alaska to California and east at least to Colorado, and farther in scattered instances.

The bright yellow water lily flower hides among the large fleshy leaves. The shiny leaf is often used as a floating rest for frogs and dragonflies.

This rootstock before cutting was near-ly the size of a basketball!

Description: Yellow water lily is a perennial aquatic plant with large fleshy leaves growing from a heavy rounded rootstock. The large rootstock has a scaly covering from the many stems that break off each winter. It somewhat resembles a green pineapple (see drawing and photographs). The stems are thick and heavy. The bright yellow flower is quite large, composed of several inward-curving petals. The seeds are shaped like small kernels of corn, darker on the outer ends.

In the field: The rootstock is more easily dug after summer dry spells lower the water level. Even so, it often is recovered only after much digging. Peel and slice the rootstock, then roast or boil it. It sometimes has a bitter taste that requires boiling in two or more waters to remove. A starchy central core is the best part, requiring less boiling to make it quite tasty. If the rootstock is not too bitter, a single boiling renders the plant ready to eat, or better still, to be recooked by frying or roasting. Boil it soft enough to mash and eat like potatoes. Or cook it into a mush and dry it as a flour in much the same manner as several other of the starchy wild rootstocks.

Collect and roast the seeds. They will pop just like popcorn, providing a remarkably similar taste, especially if eaten with melted butter and salt. You can also parch the seeds and add them to cereal or grind them into flour.

The ripe seeds are picked from inside the stiff flower.

The seeds surround the core of the water lily.

In the kitchen: The yellow water lily has good flavor and is a lot of fun to play with. After the root has been boiled enough to remove bitterness, it is ready to include in a number of excellent dishes.

PANFRIED POND LILY

WATER LILY ROOTS *2 cups sliced*

SALT *1 teaspoon*

ONION *1/4 cup finely chopped*
BUTTER *1 tablespoon*
PARSLEY

Boil the water lily roots in salt water for about 20 minutes. Drain well. In a large skillet, fry the roots and onions in butter. Garnish with chopped parsley. Simple but good. Serves 4.

PADDED DADDIES

WATER LILY ROOTS *1 cup diced*

MILK *1/4 cup*
ONIONS *1/4 cup finely chopped*
TOMATO PASTE *2 tablespoons*

CRAWFISH TAILS *12*
OIL
SALT *and* PEPPER
LEMON WEDGES

Boil the water lily roots until they are a thick mush. Stir in the milk, onion, and tomato paste until you have a thick batter. Carefully roll the peeled and boiled crawfish tails in the batter. Fry in deep fat about 5 minutes or until the batter is golden brown; season to taste. Serve with a green leafy vegetable and lemon wedges. Simply outstanding. Serves 6.

POPPALILLY

BUTTER *3 tablespoons*
RIPE WATER LILY SEEDS *1/2 cup*

SALT *1/4 teaspoon*

Allow the butter to get hot in a covered saucepan or popcorn popper. Add the seeds and shake vigorously until they are all popped. Sprinkle the salt over and serve. Makes about 2 quarts.

YERBA BUENA *(Satureja douglasii)*

This creeping little plant has collected a long and colorful history. Yerba buena, or "good herb," received its common name from early Spanish priests in California, who apparently used it as a flavoring. It had been used as a refreshing tea by the natives long before that arrival. It became a favorite of the early settlers to California and was used extensively by those who were lured to the gold fields. The rhythmic name rolled easily on the tongue, and San Francisco's first business district was known as Yerba Buena. The name still plays an important part in the place names of California.

To the north, the tea made from this attractive plant was regularly drunk by the coastal Indians as far as the Russian settlements in southeast Alaska. Although a relatively unimportant trade item, it was carried to foreign shores by the fur trappers.

Habitat and distribution: Yerba buena is strictly limited to the moist climates west of the Cascade and Sierra Mountains from British Columbia to central California.

It is found in the shade of the coniferous forest along the Pacific coast and is abundant but often overlooked along the forest floor.

Desciption: Yerba buena is a creeping vinelike plant with a woody stem. The simple leaves are opposite and may be finely haired. Tiny flowers appear in the spring and summer. They are from one-quarter- to one-half-inch long and are white, pink, or light purple. The tiny flowers growing from the leaf axils and the minty aroma of the leaves are the best characters for identification.

In the field: Collect the leaves, dry, and steep them into a refreshing tea. It has a slightly minty flavor and can be brewed quite strong. Serve cold, or hot with a drop of lemon.

In the kitchen: The only practical use of yerba buena is as a tea, but it might warrant experimentation. Like other teas, it provides little in the way of nutrition except minimal amounts of minerals. If you wanted to take the trouble to make an extract of the leaves, it might be a good flavoring for an ice cream topping or an interesting addition to a jelly.

CHAPTER 3

Fruits, Nuts, and Berries and how to make jams, jellies, and preserves

In the late summer and fall, the woods are at the height of production. Fruits, grains, seeds, and berries are abundant in every region. The advent of the autumn harvest has always been met with celebration and rejoicing. Many early civilizations considered a good harvest season a sign from a benevolent god that they could survive the coming winter without much fear. Large stores of corn, nuts, and berries were laid away with appropriate thanks and ceremonies. For many centuries, people around the world have paused to thank their own deities for the abundance that has been delivered to them. As a collector of wild edibles, it is nearly impossible to go afield during the late summer and fall without experiencing something of the same kind of awe felt by those societies that depended on the wilderness.

In the early days, the Indians made an annual trek to the mountains to collect huckleberries. At the beginning of each day's picking, they paused to give thanks to their Great Spirit, a gesture closely resembling the thanks given by a modern family at the dinner table. So important were these berry fields to the Indians that a few are still reserved for their exclusive use. In Washington's Cascades, large fields are set aside near Mount Adams for the traditional berry gathering activities of nearby tribes. It is refreshing to note that many of the old people still take part in that quiet moment each morning before they begin the day's work.

Of the plants described in this chapter, nearly all are fruits and berries. You can enjoy the few nuts included without much preparation, and they store well all winter. To take long-term advantage of the remainder of these plants, some method of preservation must be employed.

Of course, the advent of large, efficient home freezer systems has allowed us to keep the fresh flavors of the fruits and berries. Before that, canning the berries or making jams and jellies were the only ways we had to keep them. This method is still widely enjoyed, providing delightful eating throughout the winter and spring months.

There is much to be said for homemade jams and jellies. Often the commercial prime fruits are packed in the more expensive whole or sliced fruit packages, while lower grade berries become the preserves. Even so, they often have excellent flavor—imagine the superior flavor you can achieve using the finest berries.

Perhaps more important, the commercial processors pressure-cook the fruits. In so doing, they extract up to 25 percent more juice but destroy the natural pectins, so additives are included to cause the product to jell. In the open-kettle method you employ in your kitchen, the natural pectins are preserved, allowing the jelly to "set" with no outside substance added.

In the jams and jellies you make at home, about 60 percent of the whole is fruit, with 40 percent sugar added. In the commercial preparations, the law requires at least 45 percent fruit to 55 percent sugar, and the manufacturers seldom vary from that amount.

No instructions are given here for the use of commercially prepared pectins. In the unlikely event you overcook your fruit, you still don't have to add artificial or prepared pectins. Just put the jelly back in the kettle, add a few slices of pared apple, and bring to a rolling boil. Allow it to partially cool, then pour it back in your jelly jars. The high level of pectins in the apple will cause your jelly to set without the addition of a commercial product, and the flavor of your homemade jelly is not impaired.

A few fruits and berries really don't have much natural pectin in them. Unfortunately, strawberries, raspberries, and blackberries are among these. You can add one of the high-pectin fruits to these to make jelly, although it is not always necessary. The higher-pectin fruits include apples, currants, gooseberries, cranberries, and plums.

Before you begin making your jam or jelly, you can find out just how much pectin the plant contains. That determines whether you need to add any other fruit or a pectin additive, as well as how much sugar. This is important to produce a superior jam or jelly that retains the delicate flavor of the wild fruit or berry.

I learned an absolutely foolproof method of making these calculations from a lifelong friend of my grandmother's, who learned to make jelly before the turn of the century and won blue ribbons at the county fair for a great many years. At 80 years old she was still making the clearest, finest jellies I've ever tasted. Her secret was knowing *exactly* how much pectin was in the fruit, and thus how much sugar to add to each batch. Here's how she did it:

Before you begin to prepare your preserves, boil a small amount of the mashed fruit until you have extracted a teaspoonful of juice without squeezing or straining. Put the juice in a glass and allow it to cool. Add to exactly one teaspoon of juice a teaspoon of good quality 100-proof gin. Shake the glass gently. The booze will bring the pectin together in the glass in one of several ways. How the pectin reacts is the key to making your jelly, jam, or preserves the finest in the neighborhood and depends on the strength and amount available in the juice.

1. All the pectin jells into a single mass—allow one cup of sugar for each cup of fruit juice.

2. The pectin is in two or three lumps—allow two-thirds to three-fourths cup of sugar to each cup of juice, depending on the flavor of the fruit.

3. The pectin is in small beads—use one-half cup of sugar to each cup of fruit juice. A slice of apple may be required for each three cups of juice during boiling with the sugar.

4. The pectin is in tiny droplets—allow one-half cup of sugar or slightly

less per cup of fruit juice and add a slice of apple for every cup of fruit juice.

Now you are ready to proceed. I assume that you are going to make old-fashioned jams and jellies in the traditional ways, which seem to be surrounded by a certain mystique. After all, your reputation as a grandparent may hinge on your jelly-making abilities

Getting Ready: In preparing to make your own jams and jellies, you'll need three important items that aren't usually used in other cooking. First is jelly jars, either the type that has a two-piece, screw-on top or jars that have no special top and are sealed with paraffin. Wash the jars and lids and keep them good and hot until you are ready to use them.

For jelly—but not preserves, jam, or marmalade—a jelly bag is essential for producing a fine clear product. Make the bag of several layers of cheesecloth and sew it sturdily so the bag filled with fruit can be suspended over the kettle while the valuable juices drain.

Finally, the cooking kettle itself must be stainless, aluminum, or heavy enamel. Such materials as copper or iron are unsuitable. They not only change the color of many fruits, but may actually react with the acids in the fresh fruits or berries to produce a substantial toxic substance. The jam or jelly pot in the old-fashioned kitchen was invariably of heavy enamel, and I doubt that a better kettle can be found.

One added bit of preparation I find quite helpful to the making of a really superb jelly or jam is to prewarm the sugar on a large cookie sheet in a warm oven. Higher temperatures will cause the sugar to melt and be useless.

Making Jams, Jellies, and Preserves: Accurate measures, a strong stirring arm, and patience are vital in producing the fine products that will bring the family running to the breakfast table next winter. I think that cooking more than about one-and-one-half quarts of fruit or berries at one time makes the batch unmanageable, and the result is seldom as good as that produced by cooking a smaller, better controlled batch.

In making any of these fine preserves, accurate measurement of fruit, juices, and sugar is the absolute essential to making them right. Stirring the batch, especially when making jam, ensures a smooth, even mixture with a steady, deep color and uniform flavor.

About jam: Homemade jam is by far the easiest of the three and produces quite a bit more product from the same amount of fruit because it uses the berry pulp.

After you wash the berries, or peel and slice the fruit, put the bulk into the kettle, slightly crushing the bottom part of the mass to release some of the juices. If necessary, add a little water before cooking. This is usually required only if the fruit is something like apples or pears, where insufficient amounts of juice are released from the mass without cooking. In either case, the juices begin to come out as the fruit is heated.

Simmer the fruit until it is quite soft, then measure carefully before adding the prewarmed sugar. For quite sweet fruits or very ripe berries, use less than a cup of sugar to a cup of fruit. It can often be reduced by about 25 percent. (I always start with a little less sugar than I predicted from the pectin test—it's easy to add more, but tough to remove it!) Experience with a favorite fruit or berry soon tells you how much reduction is necessary.

Once the fruit mass is quite soft, pour in the sugar a little at a time, stirring constantly. (From this point on, you and your wooden spoon become inseparable partners.) Continue to stir until the sugar is well dissolved and there is no graininess to the mass of pulp.

Continuing to stir, increase the heat and bring the jam to a boil, making sure no sticking occurs. Your dexterity with the stirring spoon at this time is very important. Make sure you keep the stuff moving from all parts of the pot. Even a small burnt spot in the center of the bottom spoils flavor.

Reduce the heat and continue to cook until the jam starts to thicken. It is a good idea to have one of those heat diffuser pads to put over the heating unit during this stage to keep the heat even and not too hot. As it begins to cool, the stirring gets a bit tougher, but that's O.K. You need only stir occasionally now.

Here, patience is its own reward. Even though it may take from 30 to 45 minutes for the jam to thicken, it eventually will.

While the jam is still quite warm, take the jars from the hot water and allow them to dry for a few minutes without wiping. Pour or spoon the warm jam into the jars and seal. If you seal them right away and correctly, there is almost no chance of your hard-won treasure falling victim to mold or spoilage. I vastly prefer paraffin sealing to the patented screw-top jars, but the latter have certainly proven satisfactory for a great many people. It just seems that I haven't had a jar go bad with paraffin, while I have lost several with the two-piece lids. After all the work of collecting two or three gallons of tiny trailing blackberries, I plan to use the method that works best for me.

To seal with paraffin, be sure the upper part of the jar is thoroughly dry before adding the jam, put the seal on almost immediately, and above all, make sure the paraffin isn't too hot. Here's how:

First, cut or break the paraffin block before melting it. It becomes liquid with less time and heat. Second, and most important, NEVER melt the paraffin directly over the flame or heat. Put it in a container—a coffee can will do—and set that in a pan of hot water. It isn't necessary to boil the water if you start melting the paraffin at about the same time you start cooking the jam. Paraffin burns with a fierce flame if it is ignited, thus the precaution against getting it too hot. Furthermore, the paraffin, if quite hot, pulls away from the sides of your jelly jar, preventing an airtight seal.

Once the paraffin melts, it is permissible to allow it to cool a bit before sealing the jar. Pour about an eighth of an inch over the fresh jam and set it aside to cool. It will harden against the jam's surface, but won't adhere. Store jars in a cool place or the paraffin seal won't work. When time comes to use it, just pry the seal off.

Preserves: Making preserves or marmalades is a little more difficult than jam, but still entails only one cooking process. Preparation, however, starts the day before you intend to cook.

Although any of the wild fruits and berries are acceptable, preserves always seem better with the varieties that are more solid. Very ripe berries or plums that are getting mushy aren't as good as crab apples, firm berries, or other solid fruits.

The preserve is, essentially, a clear syrup with bits of the fruit suspended here and there throughout. The process is fairly simple and the results usually pleasing to the eye and the palate.

After testing the juice for its pectin content and determing the amount of sugar you need, place the fruit and sugar in alternate layers in the cooking kettle. Use a trifle less sugar than is required for either jam or jelly—in most cases about one-half to three-quarters of a cup of sugar per cup of mashed fruit. Cover the kettle and allow it to sit for about 24 hours. During this period the sugar and fruit begin to work together, the first step in producing a fine preserve.

On cooking day, add a little water to the kettle (about one cup for a six-cup batch of fruit) and slowly bring it to a boil. As soon as it is boiling energetically, reduce the heat and simmer until the fruit is semitransparent. Blackberries or blackcaps never quite reach this stage, but the juice has a deep translucent color. When it thickens into a syrup, it is ready to pour into the jars and seal with paraffin.

If the syrup is not thick enough, remove the majority of the fruit and set it aside, continuing to boil the liquid until it reaches the desired consistency. Gently stir the fruit back in and bottle as usual.

Clear jellies: This is probably the very finest of the homemade preserves, and the one that looks the best at the breakfast table. A jar of deep purple jelly shimmering in the morning sun looks as good as it tastes—a genuine source of enjoyment for the family and pride for the cook! It is a bit harder to accomplish, but neither mysterious nor impossible.

As with the other processes, use as little water as possible to ensure a concentrated and intense flavor. For quite dry fruits such as crab apples or volunteer pears, use a larger amount of water to get the process under way.

Crush the bottom layer of fruit gently in the cooking kettle and put the rest of the fruit on top. DO NOT ADD ANY SUGAR! Cook at a moderately low heat without stirring until quite a bit of the juice is cooked out of the fruit, then gradually increase the temperature so more of the liquid is cooked off. Keep on cooking until the fruit is very soft and begins to lose its color. As soon as the fruit is fully cooked, pour off the clear juice and put all the pulp that remains in the jelly bag. Suspend it over the kettle of clear juice and allow it to drip until you recover all of the juice. (Rinse the bag in hot water before use, wringing it out well. The damp bag does not absorb much of the juice after such treatment.)

Don't wring or squeeze the bag of pulp to try to extract more juice. The wringing action muddies the fruit juice and usually results in imparting a bitter flavor to the cooked juice. Leave well enough alone and be satisfied with what you can recover through the cooking process. The juice will be deep colored but clear—the basis for an excellent jelly.

After the juice cools, measure it carefully. From the pectin test you performed on a sample of the juice, calculate the amount of sugar you need and follow those calculations to the letter.

Bring the kettle of juice to a moderate heat and simmer for about five minutes. If any froth forms on top, skim it off. Then add the exact amount of sugar and stir continuously until it dissolves. Be very careful not to let the juice boil, which impairs the flavor and may destroy the natural pectins you worked so hard to keep. The addition of the sugar lowers the boiling point of the liquid, so watch the heat carefully. You probably have the stove on its lowest heat setting, and you may require a diffuser or sheet of asbestos to make certain it doesn't boil.

After about 10 minutes, the jelly will begin to set; that is, it is about ready to remove from the heat and put into jars. To test for readiness, allow a drop to fall into a glass of cold water. If it immediately settles to the bottom, it is done; if it spreads on the surface, it requires a little more cooking. Another way to test the jelly is to put a small amount in a cold saucer and push to see if it is beginning to set.

Pour the jelly gently into the jars so that no bubbles form. They don't hurt anything, but they don't look quite as nice. Of course, if enough air is trapped in the jelly, mold or spoilage could start from it. (Make sure the washed jars have plenty of opportunity to completely drain dry.)

Don't get alarmed if your drop of jelly in the glass of water shows it isn't ready, even after 10 or 20 minutes of cooking. Some fruits, sugar percentages, and overall amounts of jelly require cooking for as much as half an hour. Others take no more than 10 minutes altogether. Keep a close eye on the jelly so you can remove it at the correct time. Of course, the ever-present stirring spoon gets plenty of exercise during the cooking period.

These methods work for me on virtually any fruit. If there is any magic involved in the making of jams and jellies, it is in the minds of those who catch the delicate aromas issuing from your kitchen.

I particularly think of homemade jam about Christmastime. It makes a special little added gift for a very special friend. I remember a certain Christmas in Alaska. The biting cold of Christmas week had given way to the lead-gray gloom of snow clouds, and snow was falling in the driving bite of an Arctic blizzard. Among the gifts around the tree was a jar of homemade blackberry jam, sent by a thoughtful old friend. Although she certainly could not afford much, she had taken the time to think of me and send this little treasure along. With that jar came memories of hot August afternoons spent scrambling among the stumps and snags of an old logging show after the tiny berries. The lazy drone of the bees, the hot smells of fireweed and fir, the cool shade of a rest alongside a mountain stream all came flooding back. There were the blue-stained hands and a far-off afternoon in a familiar kitchen to remember. For at least a moment, the bitter cold and thousands of miles melted away, replaced by a shimmering summer long ago. It was a wonderful present, disguised as a jar of jam.

In your own kitchen you probably will work a lot harder than you thought, and you might wonder if it is all worthwhile. Come winter, the fresh flavors of the autumn berries will convince you it was. Besides, you may can a lot more than just a jar of jam! o

MOUNTAIN ASH *(Sorbus* species)

Two species of this ash are found in most mountainous areas. The sitka mountain ash *(Sorbus sitchensis)* ranges more northward than the western mountain ash *(S. occidentalis)*. Both of these trees bear large quantities of berries that are suitable for most berry purposes.

Mountain ash was a reasonably popular source among the many early Indians, who generally took advantage of all the fruits and vegetables that nature had to offer. However, it was not rated as highly as many other fruits.

The tree has one serious drawback to the collection of large numbers of the berries—location. They are generally found at elevations of about 3000 feet and higher. Sometimes you can drive there on logging roads or highway passes, but more often it entails quite a bit of hiking, which suggests a long walk lugging the fruits of your labors. In a mostly mechanized society, this has led to a definite decline in the home production of ash jellies.

WESTERN MOUNTAIN ASH *(Sorbus occidentalis)*

SITKA ASH *(Sorbus sitchensis)*

Western mountain ash has teeth only on the outer half of the leaflet.

Habitat and distribution: Mountain ash is found in moist, subalpine, and alpine environments. As a general rule, the farther north you travel, the lower the elevation at which the plant is found.

Description: Mountain ash is sometimes a tree of 30 feet in height, but more often is a shrubby bush. The leaves are pinnately compound, with 7 to 13 leaflets represented on the stem. The leaflets of both sitka and mountain ash are quite elongated. The leaflets of the sitka ash are fully toothed, but the western ash has teeth only on the outer half of the leaflet. The flowers are white, growing in large umbels at the terminus of the limbs.

The berries of the sitka ash tend to be red with a coral tint. Western ash berries are reddish with a purplish cast. The species are much more easily identified by the differences in the leaf structure.

Use: Collect very ripe berries from the lower trees. Unripe ones are too bitter to be tolerated. After a frost, the berries ripen quickly and are excellent for picking.

Although the berries are generally too sour to eat raw, they are fine when cooked, made into jams or jellies, cooked as a pie filling, or made into a fine sweet wine.

In the hunting camp, cook them into a jelly similar to cranberry that is an outstanding side to roast grouse or pheasant.

BLACKBERRIES *(Rubus* species)

TRAILING BLACKBERRY *(Rubus ursinus)*

EVERGREEN BLACKBERRY *(Rubus* species)

Easily the most widespread and abundant of all the wild berries, blackberries produce most of the fruit collected from the wild. Most common of these is the trailing blackberry *(Rubus ursinus).* The wild blackberry has

Trailing blackberry

been joined by two volunteer varieties that have escaped from cultivation and flourished in suitable habitats—the Himalaya blackberry *(R. laciniatus)* and the evergreen blackberry, which is difficult to identify by scientific name, but easy to find in the field.

The various wild blackberries made an important contribution to the diet of early Indians. Only the blue huckleberry was more widely used in the early villages.

Pioneers and settlers quickly recognized the value of these excellent berries and were able to make much greater use of them than did the Indians. The settlers brought along the knowledge of making jams and jellies, thus preserving the fruits for winter use.

A familiar scene in the frontier was repeated every fall, when large kettles of jam were cooked over open fires outside the cabins. The driest of the winter's firewood supply was committed to this important activity and small jars, crocks, and tins—among the scarcest of the pioneer housewife's supplies—were carefully saved. When a shipload of pint jars arrived in early-day Seattle, the event was headlined in the local newspapers, and the cargo brought the captain an unbelievable price.

Habitat and distribution: Trailing blackberry is found on rocky slides in the middle ranges of the mountains, creeping toward the sandy ocean beaches, twining profusely around the stumps and brush of cutover land and along the margins of the evergreen forests. It can take very dry weather but prefers the somewhat moister climates of the far North and West. A subvariety of this berry grows on the higher slopes of the mountains. Trailing blackberry produces better berries in sunny locations, but fruit is found in shady places.

Evergreen and Himalaya blackberries are generally found associated with cultivated and waste ground along roadways and fence lines and in the hardwood stands that have followed the logging of firs and pines. The long vines may climb over one another, forming an impenetrable thorny thicket. They spread rapidly and are difficult to control in cultivated areas.

Description: Trailing blackberries are identified by the alternate leaves, usually composed of three leaflets. The flowers are white and five-petaled with definite green sepals beneath. The male flower is about an inch in diameter, the female flower usually about half that size. Male and female flowers are borne on separate plants. The fruit is hard and green at first, becoming red as it matures, and finally a glossy black. It is visibly elongated with many seeds and drupelets. It often produces a reasonably large berry but has much smaller fruits during very dry seasons. In either case, the flavor is unique and delicious. The several blackberries are distinguished from the black raspberries by the fact that the fruits contain a white, pithy core. The raspberry core remains on the bush after picking.

Himalaya blackberry has rounded leaflets in alternate arrangements of three per leaf.

Himalaya blackberries are considerably larger with rounded leaflets in alternate arrangements of three per leaf. They are coarsely toothed along the margins. The thick, woody stems are armed with many recurved, stout thorns. White flowers appear in profusion, followed by berries of green, then red, and finally a purplish black when mature. The berries are larger (may measure an inch in diameter) but not as firm as the wild blackberry. The individual drupelets are glossy with a tiny hair from each. The flavor is very sweet, and they make a truly outstanding jam.

Evergreen blackberries are characterized by reddish stalks and stems and definitely pointed leaves with deep lobes. Their growing patterns are similar to those of Himalayas, and the large berries are much the same. The berries are quite firm and not as sweet as the other varieties. Their unique tart flavor makes them outstanding as a dessert and a thick jam. The evergreen and trailing blackberries freeze much better than the softer Himalaya.

These three varieties are easily distinguished by the accompanying drawings and photographs.

Evergreen blackberry has pointed leaves with deep lobes.

HIMALAYAN BLACKBERRY *(Rubus laciniatus)*

Use: Picking the berries requires a little care, since all have sharp recurved thorns along the vines and stems. Even with vast caution, you can count on lots of scratches. A good way to pick the evergreen and Himalayas from their thorny fortresses is with a ladder or large board laid over the bushes. As you walk on this support, the vines flatten under you, allowing easy access to the many large berries.

Treasure the blackberry more for excellent flavor than nutritional value. The blackberries make delicious eating out-of-hand, with milk and sugar, or stirred into hotcake batter or biscuit dough. You need not cook them in the field, but take a sizeable quantity home for jams and jellies.

CASCARA *(Rhamnus purshiana)*

Cascara is a bushy tree found in limited quantities. It is not a particularly valuable wild edible and is included here mostly for reference or when its rather unique powers are needed—its bark is one of the gentlest and most efficient laxatives to be found in the wild. The berries are edible, without the laxative effect, but they also have an unusual property: eating a substantial number turns your skin red! It might be effective if you are trying to blend in with the sunset, but otherwise is a distinct drawback.

The use of cascara as a laxative goes back as far as our records, being used by the Indians, who were often stuck with a high-fiber diet. The dried bark was crumbled into water and drunk, and the desired reaction took place a couple of hours later. Lesser amounts were recommended as a tonic and appetite-improver. For this purpose, a piece of dry bark was soaked in water overnight and the water drunk upon rising in the morning. It is reputed to be pleasant and effective.

As a seven-year-old I lived in the little logging village of Mineral, Washington. One summer day, I decided to eat a rather large quantity of the berries, which we often had eaten a few at a time. By the next morning my skin was a blotchy red, which didn't matter much because I spent most of the day in the bathroom. Needless to say, I don't really consider cascara one of my favorites!

Habitat and distribution: Cascara prefers shady woods, where it grows to a tree as much as 30 feet high. It is more often found as a spindly tree about half that size. It is found mostly west of the Cascades from Canada to California, but occurs in other suitable places.

Description: The leaves have a tendency to cluster. They are broadly oblong with rounded ends, finely toothed, glossy green above and pale green below. The bark is light gray, usually mottled with dark gray. Older trees tend to become scaly near the bottom of the trunk. The green flowers are usually inconspicuous, but the dark blue-black berries are prominent in the late summer and fall.

Use: Cascara berries are fine if eaten in small amounts, but they are pretty tasteless and have a large number of seeds. It is kind of fun to eat a few while you are in the field, but I doubt that you would take a bucketful home for jam. They just aren't very tasty. The bark is a fine laxative if needed. Dry the bark and mix with water, or boil the green bark.

Cascara

CHOKECHERRY *(Prunus virginiana)*

The several varieties of chokecherry are common in at least one form throughout, particularly in drier regions. Chokecherry ripens earlier than many other wild fruits, so it is valuable to collect and preserve before the bulk of the berries are ready.

The chokecherries were very popular with many Indian groups. They were usually cooked and pitted before eating, but were not easily preserved. Modern methods of making jellies and preserves have made them a lot more valuable.

There is a certain danger to chokecherries—along with related domestic plants including apricots, peaches, and bitter almonds—that lies in the pits. All contain dangerous levels of cyanide. There have been authenticated cases of serious poisonings and deaths attributed to the ingestion of chokecherry seeds. There is reason to be careful with the seeds of all these plants.

Chokecherries hang in long clusters.

Habitat and distribution: The several varieties are found in damp places or wet ground in all parts of the country. They are not abundant on the coastal plain, but are found in large numbers elsewhere throughout the West.

Description: Chokecherry may occur as a large bush or a small tree, usually not more than 20 feet high. The leaves are cherrylike, finely toothed on the margins, and larger above the middle than below it. Two small glands are located on the leaf stems just below the leaf. The flowers are white and appear in large trailing clusters. The fruits are small and numerous. Usually smaller than one-half-inch in diameter, they are a dark purple when ripe. Even ripe, they are very sour, but make fine preserves.

Use: You can eat a few fruits raw and they are quite refreshing, but a few are enough. Their tart sourness is a bit overpowering. They are best taken home and processed into jam or a very superior jelly.

Never eat the seeds, as they contain fairly high concentrations of cyanide. The leaves also contain this toxin so leave them alone. Cyanide is an oily, volatile poison that is released by cooking. If you are making jellies or preserves, it is best to remove the pits before cooking, but not very practical. The accepted method is to partially cook the cherries, remove the pits, and then proceed with the very thorough cooking needed for making jelly. It makes a little extra work, but the fine flavor of the jelly and the added safety of the method makes it worthwhile. Chokecherries are not particularly nutritious.

OREGON CRAB APPLE *(Malus* species)

The Oregon crab apple, sometimes known as Pacific crab apple, has a detailed history as a food item, but I won't try to list all its older usages. It is one of those wild edibles that never seems to cause any kind of prejudice, since it looks and tastes something like the cultivated apple.

It is important to note that the crab apple may have been the forerunner of cultivation for many native groups, since they found that if they cut off the "suckers"—the upright limbs—the tree would produce more fruit the following season. A few old records indicate that the women regularly pruned the trees in their usual gathering grounds. This practice probably would have led ultimately to the establishment of a husbandry program of sorts, had not the white man interrupted the progress of Indian culture.

Habitat and distribution: Oregon crab apple is limited to the west side of the Cascades and Sierras and extends from central California to Alaska. It prefers moist ground where it is protected by other trees. It is especially abundant in woodlots and thickets that are not being reclaimed by the giant conifers of these regions.

OREGON CRAB APPLE *(Malus* species)

Oregon crab apple has sprays of blossoms.

Description: A small tree, Oregon crab apple often assumes a gnarled and twisted posture. The leaves are alternate, pointed, and finely toothed. They are occasionally slightly lobed and resemble the cultivated apple. The white flowers grow in flat clusters. The fruits are typically applelike and oval but quite small.

Use: Pick crab apples from the tree and eat them raw or cooked, or make them into excellent pies, jellies, and preserves. Because of a high level of natural pectin, it is additionally valuable for adding to jellies. If the fruits are fully ripe, they have a good enough flavor, but slightly green ones are almost unbearably sour. They are especially good if baked in the coals of a campfire, which softens and sweetens the fruit. You can store them in a cool place for fairly long periods before cooking into jellies.

NOTE: Never eat crab apple seeds. As with all apples, the cyanide content of the seeds is quite high. There have been cases recorded of human deaths from eating a fair quantity of apple seeds. Remove them during cooking or bypass them when eating the fruit raw.

CRANBERRY *(Vaccinium oxycoccus)*
HIGHBUSH CRANBERRY *(Viburnum opulus)*

CRANBERRY *(Vaccinium oxycoccus)*

HIGHBUSH CRANBERRY *(Viburnum opulus)*

Although these two plants are not even related, the fruits are almost identical in form, flavor, and composition. For that reason, they are dealt with as a single unit. They are handled in all the same ways.

The cranberry never achieved much popularity among the Indians except a few groups along the eastern seaboard. When the first white men came to North America, however, they quickly adopted the plant and began making fine jellies and sauces from it. It is a berry that is virtually impossible to eat raw, which helps explain its lack of success with the early Indians.

The northeastern Indians boiled large quantities of cranberries with the sap from a sugar maple and allowed the mass to cool. Chunks of the jellied sauce were wrapped in leaves and carried as they traveled, providing a welcome change from the typical diet along the trail.

Habitat and distribution: The low-lying cranberry plant nearly always seeks wet bogs and acid soils. It is expressly suited to the conditions quite near the ocean beaches. The low species is widely cultivated on both coasts and grows in immense numbers in the subarctic tundra of Canada and Alaska. It is found along the northern half of the Pacific Coast.

Highbush cranberry is much more widely distributed, occurring in most of the western states in suitable situations. It is generally found along stream banks and in well-watered soils. This plant is reasonably widespread in southern Canada, but decreases in range as you proceed southward.

Description: Cranberry is a thin creeping vine up to about 48 inches in length, seldom venturing up out of the moss in which it grows. The leaves are tiny, pointed, and nearly stemless. They are alternate, evergreen, and may have almost invisible teeth. The flowers are white, pinkish, or red. The shiny fruit is white, becoming red as it ripens.

Highbush cranberry is a large, upright bush that is readily identified by the very distinctive bell-shaped leaves. Often the upright stems lie low to the ground, making this plant more difficult to find. White flowers appear in small umbels at the terminus of the stems. The fruit is bright red and closely resembles the other cranberry in shape and flavor.

Use: These cranberries contain an inordinate amount of pectin, causing them to jell after a simple boiling. Pick and lightly boil the berries, then allow then to jell. If sugar is available, add it during cooking to sweeten the sauce. Cook with almost no water, as you would a fruit for jam. It is an excellent dish in the hunting camp to complement a fresh venison liver or a grouse.

CROWBERRY *(Empetrum nigrum)*

Crowberry is widespread but relatively unnoticed. Coastal Indians used it in many ways; recent archaeological finds have indicated that at least a few isolated villages used the fermented juice as a sort of beer. The beer is simple to make and supposedly a pretty effective intoxicant. It was used in a more or less ceremonial manner, generally before a party left the village on a hunt or exploring mission. Although it was reputed to have properties that increased the bravery of the members, it probably just got them a little drunk, thereby tranquilizing them slightly. (That custom seems to be increasing in popularity in all societies!)

Crowberry was also used in the manufacture of an unusual wine that became quite popular among white settlers to the Northwest. Early records show that it was made in substantial quantities in a few places. On Washington's Olympic Peninsula this wine was used as a trade item for a short time. In the late 1800s a group of Scandinavian settlers along the Quinault and Humptulips rivers made this wine from the abundant berries and traded for Indian staple foods, helping them survive a couple of tough winters. A scattered handful of old families in that area still make a sweet, clear wine.

As a table fruit, crowberry is a little hard to get used to. It never gained great popularity as a raw berry, even among the Indians, but is eagerly sought by birds and animals.

CROWBERRY *(Empetrum nigrum)*

Habitat and distribution: Crowberry is widely distributed throughout the mountains and coastal areas, wherever rainfall is high enough and the soil is damp. They seem to prefer the slightly acid soils of the coast. They are found from California into southcentral Alaska and are especially common along the Washington and British Columbia coastal belts.

Description: Crowberry is a low, ground-covering plant, similar in habitat and appearance to the heathers. The leaves are thick and shiny, somewhat resembling the needles of a fir tree. They are usually about one-quarter-inch long in rough whorls about the many branches and upright stems.

The tiny blossoms are purple and inconspicuous. The berries are waxy black, smooth, and quite plentiful on the low bushes. The plant seldom grows over six inches tall, but may spread over large areas, especially in the shade of larger trees or undergrowth.

Use: Crowberry has a unique flavor that is not particularly popular but can become appreciated with familiarity. They are best cooked into a quick jam or sauce and served over biscuits or hotcakes. The raw berries may also be turned into hotcake batter to make a good dish.

Make a simple beer by crushing the berries and adding a bit of water and dark molasses or brown sugar. Cap tightly in airtight containers and allow to ferment for a few days. Strain and cool the juice before use. It develops a fair alcohol content.

Their best use is in jams, jellies, and homemade wines.

WILD CURRANT *(Ribes* species)

(color photo, page 174)

A dozen or so wild currants and gooseberries are found in many different situations, and they are all treated in this section since they are similar in appearance and uses.

The berries of currant grow upward.

The early Indians used the currants in the production of a potent wine that was often reserved for ceremonial purposes. The fruits were also made into very tart sauces, but the Indians had not yet learned to make sweetened jams and jellies.

When the early settlers came, they quickly adopted the plant for making a fine sweet wine. They also made large quantities of currant and gooseberry jams and preserves. The manufacture of currant wines is an integral part of the wine industry in many parts of the Northwest today, although the bushes are cultivated. These bushes, however, sprang from some of the species that are presently found in the wild.

Habitat and distribution: The currants and gooseberries prefer moist conditions but are found in creek bottoms and gullies in even the semiarid sections. They prosper in thickets along the streams in wetter sections of the country and can easily grow in brushland and unused land. At least a few bushes are usually found in any area.

Description: The currants are characterized by single leaves that because of the deep lobes appear to be three to seven leaflets depending on the species. They are toothed, notched, òr entire.

The flowers are white, greenish, pink, or red. The fruits are green, yellow, red, or nearly black, but are often semitransparent. The fruits often have a whitish waxy bloom over the skin.

There is a slight difference in the appearance of the fruits in some cases, and one difference between gooseberries and currants makes distinction immediate: the gooseberries all have spines or stickers, while the currants are unarmed. Their uses are quite the same.

Use: The fruits of the currants and gooseberries are edible raw but are seldom used this way because of their sourness or tartness, verging on becoming bitter. Occasionally, very ripe fruit becomes pleasantly sweetish. The berries are excellent for jams and jellies and make a superior wine, which has long been favored. The gooseberries make a particularly fine filling for pies.

NOTE: The fruit of one species, *Ribes viscosissimum,* is inedible. It can cause violent vomiting shortly after ingesting the currants. This plant differs from the others in having a sticky substance on the leaves, twigs, and fruits. Because of this, it is commonly called the sticky currant. It is best identified by the few fruits that are covered with short bristly hairs that make it quite unappetizing.

The glossy berries appear under the typical three-lobed leaves. The remnants of the blossoms hang from these immature fruits.

PACIFIC DOGWOOD *(Cornus nuttallii)*

The western or flowering dogwood is a rather large tree that produces big showy flowers in the spring. Even though they aren't technically flowers, they are easy to find and identify.

In the fall, the tree produces clusters of scarlet berries that are edible, but tasteless and without character. The berries were never very popular among the early Indians as a food, but the tree was useful in other ways. The leaves and inner bark were dried as an important addition to ceremonial smoking mixtures, while the bark had several medicinal uses. It was reportedly used as a tonic for colds and fever. This use may have had some value, since the fresh bark is something of a cathartic. It is strong enough to be less a laxative than a product that causes diarrhea. Although a few early medical texts prescribe it as a tonic, it apparently didn't gain widespread use.

The glossy dogwood leaves support the showy flowers.

PACIFIC DOGWOOD *(Cornus nuttallii)* color photo, page 166

Dogwood flower.

Habitat and distribution: Flowering dogwood appears along the coastal regions from British Columbia into California but seldom is found east of the Cascade range. It thrives in a variety of soils and is especially prevalent along roadsides and in thick brushland.

Description: Flowering dogwood is best identified by the large white flowers that cover the tree during the spring. They are composed of a tightly packed cluster of small green flowers surrounded by four to six large bracts. The leaves are glossy green on top and much whiter below. They are opposite and feature characteristic veins that curve parallel to the outer edge of the leaf. In the fall the leaves may have a reddish tint.

The scarlet bell-shaped berries form from the tight central flower, leaving a roundish cluster on short stems.

Use: The berries are the most important part, but are not a particularly valuable food. You can eat the berries raw or cooked, but they are not terribly flavorful. Make into jams and jellies, but add apple or some other fruit since the berries are bland and contain little pectin.

Crush the dried bark and mix with water to produce a tonic that is good after the bark has soaked for several hours. The strength of the tonic varies widely with the individual tree.

BLUE ELDERBERRY *(Sambucus cerulea)*

Although the elderberry is certainly a wild plant, it has been used for wines, jams, and preserves for hundreds of years. Three major species are found throughout, two of which are edible. The third, the red elderberry, is reputed to be poisonous, and several cases of severe poisoning have been attributed to it.

Two early uses for the darker berries are recorded by the Indians. They cooked the juice from the blue and black varieties to make wine and used the bark for medicinal purposes. It was supposed to be a diuretic and purgative, but overdoses were apparently experienced by the patient that could lead to death. The bark long ago fell from favor as a folk medicine because of the wide variations in strength of the extracts. As a wine, however, it has remained popular. Commercially prepared wines, jams, and jellies are made from blue elderberries in several sections of the country.

5 TO 9 LEAFLETS

BLUE ELDERBERRY *(Sambucus cerulea)* color photo, page 174

Blue elderberries.

Habitat and distribution: Elderberry is a common roadside plant in moist sections. It prefers stream banks and low to middle elevations, but is found in almost any sort of brushland or unused ground. Along many of the mountain streams in the north and west sections, it is the predominant plant. It isn't widely cultivated because it manages to grow abundantly in almost all areas of the country.

Description: The easiest differentiation between the species is in the color of the berry, which is the edibility key. Reddish berries are not edible, but blue, black, or bluish-black ones are excellent. The elderberry is a large bush or small tree, sometimes growing to more than 20 feet. The leaves are pinnately compound, pointed, and sharply toothed; they usually are in compound leaves of nine leaflets, but five or seven are not uncommon. The woody stalks and stems are filled with a fine pithy substance. The flowers of all types are white to cream colored and carried in large terminal racemes. The fruits are globose. The nutlets are rough and wrinkled.

Use: You can pick the berries from the tree in large numbers. Raw, the blue and black berries may cause gastric disturbances. They are far better cooked into jam or jelly or made into a sweet wine. A couple of cups of berries cooked well and allowed to jell make a fine tart sauce that goes well with a camp dinner of roasted grouse or venison.

OREGON FAIRY BELLS *(Disporum oreganum)*

The various fairy bells are beautiful additions to our forests, shyly hiding under the spreading leaves of the plant. A few authorities have recently questioned the edibility of the fruits, but experience and history have shown them to be edible. Several large Indian groups used them rather extensively, and they are occasionally found in the twentieth-century kitchen.

The earliest use for the plant was simply as a raw fruit eaten off the vine, and as such it was quite popular. The flavor often isn't as great as you'd like, so they are soon relegated to the cooking pot for a fine and flavorful jelly.

Habitat and distribution: Fairy bells are usually found in rich, moist soils under the protective canopies of the evergreen forest, but occasionally may be found at the margins of the forest and alongside roadways.

OREGON FAIRY BELLS *(Disporum oreganum)* color photo, page 163

Although the leaves resemble false Solomon's seal, the many branched stems identify the Oregon fairy bell.

Description: Fairy bells have low, angled, many-branched stems with horizontal leaves arranged alternately along the stems. The leaves are glossy green, parallel veined, entire, and pointed at the apex. The bell-shaped white flowers hang below the leaves and are partially hidden by them. When the fruits appear, they are yellow or orange, oblong, and somewhat velvety to the touch.

Use: If the fruits are ripe, they are excellent when eaten raw, but those that are slightly green have a terribly sour flavor. At this stage they are good for jams and jellies. The pectin content of fairy bells varies greatly, so a pectin test is almost essential before making your home preserves. The ripe berries make a sweet sauce in the camp that is boiled, allowed to set, and served with meat as you would cranberries. In places where the berries are found in quantity, they make a delicious fruit filling for pies or baked rolls.

HAZELNUT *(Corylus cornuta)*

One of the few native edible nuts, the hazelnut was long a favorite of the Indians, the settlers who followed, and families that have lived here ever since. If they are found, hazelnuts are among the most delicious of all nuts, whatever their source. Unfortunately, they are also quite popular with squirrels, chipmunks, and a lot of other forest creatures who are liable to beat the rest of us to them. Even some birds can cope with the hard shells.

The hazelnut is commercially cultivated under the name filbert and commands a high price in the market. It is generally used simply as a nutmeat to be eaten out-of-hand, but it has many other uses in the modern home.

The early Indians quickly recognized the advantages of this fine nut as a flour and ground great quantities of it for baking. Once ground, the flour kept for long periods without spoiling, but mice and other rodents eagerly sought it. Some early cultures built rather elaborate and complex storage facilities to protect their hazelnut flours—which was certainly warranted, as it was nutritious and easily ground.

The hazelnut has more calories per hundred grams than beefsteak, pure sugar, or even chocolate cake! In a survival situation, it is among the first you'd want to find. These nuts are also important in obtaining fats and proteins from the wild pantry.

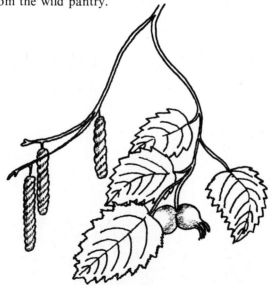

HAZELNUT *(Corylus cornuta)* color photo, page 166

Habitat and distribution: One of the two major types of hazelnut is probably found in suitable ground anywhere except the desert sections. They prefer lower elevations, below 2500 feet, but are occasionally found higher. The largest concentrations are west of the Cascade range from California into British Columbia.

Description: Hazelnuts are the fruits of a small tree or large shrub that is spreading and seldom over 20 feet high. The leaves are rounded, uniformly toothed, and pale beneath. They are strongly veined and alternate. The bush is easily distinguished in the spring when yellow catkins appear hanging in the old leaf axils. These are twisted, slender growths that soon fall from the tree. The nuts are sheathed by a ragged pair of bracts that form a stocking. Inside, the hard, thin shells protect the meat.

Use: Hazelnuts are easy to pick and crack. Usually two nuts are found on each stem, although singles or threes are not uncommon. Eat them raw, grind them into a fine white flour, or roughly grate them and add to cake or cookie batter. A favorite way of using these nuts is to grate or grind them and add the result to stone-ground cereals as a breakfast food. Ground hazelnuts, dried fruits, and cereal grains make one of the most delicious and nutritionally valuable foods you could possible prepare.

The nuts are best if dried for a few days before use. Store a fresh bag of hazelnuts until Christmas, when they become part of the traditional dressing, a fine addition to biscuits, and a treat when cracked and eaten alone.

The soft texture of the leaves identify the beaked hazelnut, enclosed in the hairy stocking.

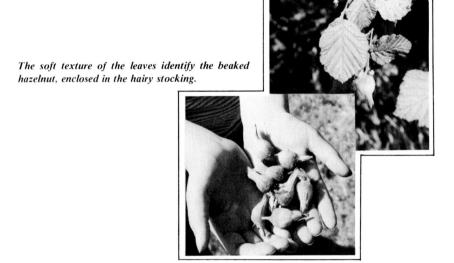

ORANGE HONEYSUCKLE *(Lonicera ciliosa)*

"CUPPED" END LEAF

This beautiful flower is very visible during the spring, when large tubular orange flowers appear, brightening the forests and woodlands, It then fades into the background until fall, when the lovely orange berries appear in small clusters.

Honeysuckle apparently did not have an important place in the diets of the early Indians, although several records indicate they were used on some occasions. The reason for their lack of use was probably the plant's relative scarcity then. Following the advent of industrial logging development, conditions for this wiry shrub improved greatly, and it is much more abundant in the wild than it was a few decades ago. The pleasant-tasting fruit is now readily available throughout the mountainous regions and is collected without much difficulty.

Habitat and distribution: Orange honeysuckle and its relatives are found throughout the lower elevations. It often grows in association with cascara, thimbleberry, and salmonberry. It is therefore most abundant in moist, shady places, particularly along riverbanks and wooded roadsides.

Description: Orange honeysuckle is a vinelike shrub that usually climbs on larger plants. The leaves are oval, entire, and opposite. There is a whitish powdery bloom on the underside that easily rubs off and is a good identifier of the honeysuckles. The flowers are tube-shaped, bright orange, and located in a unique sheath at the end of each stem. The sheaths are actually two terminal leaves that have joined to make a funnel-shaped cup. The berries which appear in the sheath develop at different rates, with three or four dominant berries.

Use: Honeysuckle berries are excellent raw, if fully ripened, or made into jams and jellies. They are outstanding if a handful is mixed with your hotcake batter for breakfast. They are reputed to make a fine wine, but I have never tasted it. From the delicate sweet flavor, it could easily be true.

My favorite use for orange honeysuckle is to pick a handful while I am trout fishing and eat them slowly as I dawdle along a particularly lovely stretch of the stream. It is a restful and refreshing departure from the serious business of outwitting the wily trout.

Orange honeysuckle flowers are located in a unique sheath at the end of each stem.

260

HUCKLEBERRY *(Vaccinium* species)

RED HUCKLEBERRY *(Vaccinium parvifolium)*

BLUE HUCKLEBERRY *(Vaccinium ovalifolium)*

At least one of the dozen or more species of huckleberry is found growing wild virtually everywhere, except for the deserts. Some are now extensively cultivated under the common name blueberries. At least half the wild

Red huckleberry leaves do not turn as red or brown as those of blue huckleberry.

Blue huckleberry leaves are glossy green, becoming reddish and purple late in the season.

huckleberries are often called blueberry, grouseberry, or bilberry in some regions. Whatever the name, they are delicious small berries that can be used in a number of ways.

Among the early Indians, the blue-leaved huckleberry *(Vaccinium deliciosum)* was perhaps the most important of all wild berries. During the fall, whole tribes trekked to the mountainous fields of blue huckleberries, where they spent up to a month at the harvest. The huckleberry season marked a time of much social contact, competitive sports, and a "carnival" atmosphere. In one of the larger berrying places near Washington's Mt. Adams, the tribes met each season for centuries. Gambling, trading, and pony racing were as much a part of the activity as gathering the berries. In one meadow nearby there is a straight race course that has been worn more than a foot deep by thousands of pony hooves over the years. It is now set aside as a landmark in one of our national forests.

To these early residents, the huckleberry was a source of dried fruit, sweet sauces, jams, wine, and an individual fried pie that is delicious. When the white settlers came, they immediately saw the value of these abundant berries and quickly incorporated them into the household diet. Except for blackberries, no other wild fruit played such an important part in the menu of the pioneers.

Habitat and distribution: Huckleberries are found in moist or mountainous areas. Many of the blue varieties grow at higher elevations, but a few are found down to sea level. The red are prominent along the coasts and lower elevation streams. The most important species, delicious blueberry, is found in alpine and subalpine settings.

Description: Huckleberries vary in form, ranging from low vinelike bushes to upright many-branched shrubs. They all have small, alternate leaves that are entire or lightly toothed. Often the leaves are dark green above and whitish below. The flowers are urn-shaped and usually pinkish or white. The glossy round berries are red, blue-black, or blue. Some plants are evergreen, while others are deciduous, depending on the species.

Like most berries, wild huckleberries don't rate very high nutritionally.

Use: They are excellent to gather and eat raw or cook into sauces, jams, jellies, and especially pies. In the field camp, mix the berries with sugar, fold into a half-moon of dough, and fry to make an individual pie that is really a treat. Add them whole to hotcake or biscuit dough to give a fine sweet flavor. The plump red berries are much better made into jellies or jams than eaten raw.

KINNIKINNICK *(Arctostaphylos uva-ursi)*

This important wild berry, often called bearberry, is suited to a variety of novel uses. Over the years, it has traditionally been drunk, smoked, and eaten raw or cooked. The common name kinnikinnick is taken directly from an Indian dialect and means "smoking plant." For this purpose, the leaves were partially dried and cut into small pieces. As a tobacco substitute, kinnikinnick makes a fine mild smoke.

These were important berries to the Indians, who dried them into large cakes and used them in pemmican, a dried meat product that kept well and was carried along on hunting parties. The dried cakes were an intertribal trade item that brought high prices during years of poor berry growth.

Kinnikinnick is a close relative of the several varieties of manzanita that are found throughout. Use manzanita berries in all the same ways, but the leaves are unsuitable for smoking. Manzanita bark, on the other hand, has medical applications that are not shared by kinnikinnick.

Habitat and distribution: Kinnikinnick is the most widespread of this genus, found from sea level to the middle elevations from California to Alaska and eastward through the Rockies. Other related species grow in all areas except the deserts, but may even occur on the fringes of extreme desert.

Description: Kinnikinnick is generally a low spreading bush, but may reach the size of a small tree under ideal conditions. The leaves are tough and leathery, small, and usually finely toothed. They are alternate on the many

The tiny, leathery leaves of kinnikinnick hide hundreds of small blossoms. Young berries are forming along the margins of the stems.

small limbs and twigs, generally in a horizontal plane. The tiny white flowers are quite distinctively bell-shaped. The blackish berries grow in profusion along the outer limbs.

Use: You can eat kinnikinnick raw, but the berries are much better after cooking. They make excellent jams, jellies, pies, and wines. Dry the berries and combine with grated nuts and grains for an outstanding breakfast dish.

Bearberry cider is a popular drink made by crushing the berries and boiling them for a few minutes, just until the seeds are soft. To a quart of the cooked berries and juice, add a quart of water. Allow it to settle for several hours and pour off the resultant juice. It is refreshing and delicious, and quite likely could be allowed to ferment, if desired.

For smoking, allow the leaves to dry for a few hours, then crush. The very dry leaves that are often found on one or more limbs of a healthy bush are a bit too hot to smoke, but the partially dried leaves make a mild tobacco substitute without much bite.

The bark supposedly has astringent and diuretic properties, but probably isn't terribly reliable for this purpose.

KINNIKINNICK *(Arctostaphylos uva-ursi)* color photo, page 174

MADRONA *(Arbutus menziesii)*

The madrona is a colorful tree familiar to anyone who lives along the lower coastal elevations. It is characterized by reddish bark that seems to be in the constant process of peeling. Since the leaves and bark make a terrible mess under the tree, it is seldom used as an ornamental and is the bane of many homeowners.

For many years, the story has circulated that the berries from the madrona are poisonous. It is difficult to tell where or when it all started, but reputable newspapers have carried stories of severe poisoning cases attributed to it. Checks with poison agencies and hospitals showed this reputation is unearned. Many people have eaten the berries for a great many years without any difficulty. Some bands of Indians used the berries and dried them for use in pemmican. I have eaten madrona from time to time over the years with no ill effects, although I must admit they are not particularly flavorful raw.

One isolated tribe in western Washington made the berries into a kind of fruit beer, an art that is still carried on today. The berries were crushed and boiled. The mass of pulp and juice was combined with an equal amount of water, tightly capped, and allowed to ferment. Although the taste leaves a bit to be desired, the kick is definitely included in this firewater brew!

The flower will appear in the middle of the upright cluster of new madrona leaves.

MADRONA *(Arbutus menziesii)*

Habitat and distribution: Madrona grows quite well in the wild and is particularly abundant along the shores of Puget Sound and the Pacific Coast from central British Columbia into California. It also extends inland for many miles along major rivers.

Madrona bark peels year round.

Description: Madrona is an irregular tree of up to two feet in diameter that grows into a generally rounded shape if not crowded by other trees. The leaves are tough and leathery with very glossy upper sides. They are oval to oblong and entire, with a prominent central vein. Creamy bell-shaped flowers appear in early spring, followed by masses of orange-red berries. The berries are quite seedy by most standards. They are often nearly a half-inch in diameter. The bark of the tree peels and drops off in ragged scales, revealing a smooth, red inner surface. Young shoots often appear around the trunks of the larger trees.

Use: While not a particularly valuable wild berry, in some areas it is abundant enough to warrant a try in the kitchen at berrying time. Collect the berries from low limbs and smaller trees. Although they are edible when raw, they are much better if cooked and the seeds strained out. For this reason, they are best in jellies and wines. You can dry the cooked berries into cakes for later use.

OAKS *(Quercus* species)

OAK *(Quercus garryana)*

Nearly 40 different oak trees range across the continent, and all produce a very similar nut, the acorn. While all these acorns are edible, some are more edible than others.

All the acorns contain a certain amount of tannin. In some, it is not enough to make any difference, while in others the tannin content is high enough to cause some gastric disorder. In species with little tannin, you can eat the acorns raw or simply roasted, while those with higher contents require some method of leaching the tannin out. The latter process, even though it produces a perfectly safe result, is a lot of bother. It is better to choose those that are edible in their natural state.

But here we run up against another problem. The differences between the various trees and acorns are so slight that it takes an experienced forester or botanist to accurately identify each species.

Various Indian communities developed rather ingenious methods for making the acorns safe that the collector can easily follow today. In almost every case, the shelled acorns were ground into a meal and the tannin leached from it, which was easier than from whole nuts, although some tribes even did that.

Most often, the meal was placed in a mesh bag, tightly woven of fibrous grasses or vines. It was suspended in running water to allow the tannin to be carried away, while the meal remained in the bag. It was kneaded every so often to speed up the process. A full day's treatment in this fashion resulted in a rather bleached, safe meal which was used for making nutritious, delicious cakes.

Another quite effective method was to put the meal in tightly woven baskets and pour boiling water over it. The meal remained in the baskets and the tannin was carried through the weave, but the method called for inordinate amounts of hot water, heated under rather primitive conditions.

You can see why it's best to choose acorns that are low in tannin. If you can readily identify Gambel's oak, it is quite safe. The Garry oak is also reputed to be safe to eat, but that has not been positively substantiated. (I have eaten the acorns from the Garry oak in small numbers. I had no trouble with them, but the test was inconclusive since I ingested only a few at once.)

The acorns produced by white oaks are usually superior to those of black oaks, but there is no hard and fast general rule. It is best to consult a local reference about the oaks found where you plan to collect wild edibles. If you have the slightest doubt, put the nuts through some sort of leaching process to be safe.

Habitat and distribution: Nearly all the three dozen species of oak are found somewhere, in habitat that ranges from very moist to very dry. The range of elevation is from sea level to mountainsides. It is impossible to pinpoint any specific locales, since they grow practically everywhere.

Description: The oaks range from shrubby bushes to gigantic trees. They are evergreen or deciduous, but usually have the characteristic deeply lobed oak leaf. The "live oak" species may vary from that leaf pattern, so consult a handbook on trees for a specific region. The most reliable identification of the group is the acorn, recognizable by almost anyone.

Use: Collect the acorns from the ground under oak trees. Check them closely for tiny worm holes, especially in late fall. Many people have carried home a sackful, only to be disappointed by finding nothing inside the shells except a few well-fed worms.

You can eat many species raw or roasted, but many others require a treatment to remove the tannins. The traditional Indian methods outlined above are probably the most efficient for a simple field application. By using a good cloth bag to hold the meal and letting it soak in moving water for 24 hours, you are assured of a fine product.

Acorn meal is excellent when included in biscuits and hotcakes and is a tasty addition to soups and stews. Dry or roast it also and add to cereal and fruits as a fine breakfast food.

Fallen oak leaves

OCEAN SPRAY *(Holodiscus discolor)*

Ocean spray is a widespread flowering shrub that almost everyone has seen in large numbers and completely overlooked. It is abundant along roadsides throughout the northern and western parts of the country.

Ocean spray does not seem a likely candidate for a wild edible, having no really discernible fruit, but it actually provides a lot of good eating. Although the shrub was an important food item to the early Indians, it never achieved much popularity with the white settlers, and in later years seemed to drop completely from favor. Not even many of those who have tried to keep the art of foraging alive have recognized the possibilities of this unusual little tree.

It produces a great many little single-seeded fruits that seem more like tiny nuts than berries. The Indians most often ate these fruits raw as they became ripe, but they also cooked, ground, or dried the fruits. Because of the physical impossibility of removing the seeds in large numbers, the native people made dishes that allowed the seeds to be eaten along with the fruits. There is little known about just what kind of foods they prepared, but in at least a few communities they collected the berries in large numbers.

Habitat and distribution: Ocean spray is found in a wide range of environmental conditions at the lower elevations, choosing dry land and damp riverbanks with the same ease. It is found widely in the three coastal states, Idaho, Montana, and British Columbia, and occasionally in Alberta, Wyoming, and Colorado.

Ocean spray showing a triangular husk.

OCEAN SPRAY *(Holodiscus discolor)*

Description: Ocean spray is a many-branched shrub or small tree up to 20 feet in height. The deciduous leaves are very triangular, with a definite wedge at the lower end. The plant bears many foamy racemes of white flowers at the terminus of the stems (hence the name). The triangular husks often remain through the winter as an added identifier. The fruits are one-seeded, small, and hard, with a straight upper line and a convex lower edge.

Use: The fruits are relatively easy to collect and prepare. Strip the many small fruits from the bushes and separate from their stems and eat them raw or cooked. With some effort you can make them into jams or jellies, but they probably are best used as a simple food in the field.

OREGON GRAPE *(Berberis* species)

This is one of our most familiar ground-covering bushes, difficult to mistake for any other. Regionally known as barberry or mahonia, the Oregon grape was an important source of food for early settlers traveling by wagon over the Oregon Trail, hence the name.

The first people to inhabit the western part of the continent greatly appreciated this berry. It was readily available, had a fine taste, and could be made into a variety of outstanding products.

At least three kinds thrive in suitable places, but the differences are usually in the overall shape of the plant. The fruits are identical and are identically used. Oregon grape is an altogether too familiar plant to spend a lot of time worrying about identification or its history.

Habitat and distribution: Oregon grape is found in habitats ranging from · dry to moist, at most elevations except alpine, and in either shaded or sunny situations. It ranges from California to Alaska and eastward throughout the western United States and Canada.

Description: The Oregon grapes are easily distinguished by the prickly, hollylike leaves that are characteristic of all of them. The plants may vary from a creeping vine to a tall upright shrub, but the leaves, flowers, and berries are all the same.

Bright yellow clusters of flowers appear in the spring, followed by small berries or "grapes." These fruits are bright blue to purple, with a waxy outer skin that often gives the skin a powdery white frosted look.

Use: Pluck the ripe berries from the bushes and eat them raw or cooked. These juicy berries are excellent for making jams, jellies, and a pleasant sweet wine. As a pie filling, Oregon grape is a bit overpowering. Mixed with equal parts of apple, though, it is a fine filling, especially for breakfast rolls.

The tall variety, mahonia.

274

Trailing variety of Oregon grape.

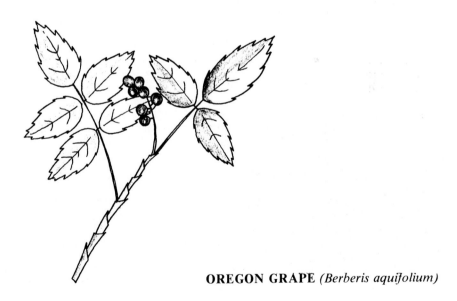

OREGON GRAPE *(Berberis aquifolium)*

PINE NUTS *(Pinus* species)

The various pines are widespread. The best of the edible species are the pinon and nut pine of the dry mountains in the Southwest.

Most of the pines bear edible seeds within the cones, but the smaller varieties of cone aren't worth the effort to get the seeds out. In most cases, the fallen cone has already released the seeds, so only those still clinging to the limbs of the tree contain the edible nuts.

One word of warning, though: DON'T try cutting down a tree to get at the cones. The trees are either on private property or on government-owned land, and the penalties for cutting down trees without proper authorization are severe.

Habitat and distribution: As a group, the pines are spread virtually everywhere on the continent. The better species are found in the drier parts of the country, particularly the Southwest. Check a local tree identification book for help in identifying species in your vicinity.

Description: The pines are large trees, characterized by long needles borne in bundles, rather than singly as in firs, hemlocks, and spruces. The barks are rough and scaly, ranging from gray to reddish depending on the species.

The cones usually are composed of a great many woody bracts with a single, sharp spine curving downward from each. The nuts are enclosed in winged husks and are between the layers of bracts.

Use: You can laboriously pick a few pine nuts from a ripe cone, shell, and eat them raw, but the effort is more than the reward warrants. It is better to collect the cones containing ripe seeds and extract them by putting the cones on a screen and allowing them to dry naturally. In a few days shake them and all the nuts will fall out. Sear off the wings and husks in an open flame and eat the clean nuts whole or grind them into a meal or flour to make nutritious biscuits or cakes that contain large amounts of protein and food energy. The nuts are also an excellent natural breakfast when mixed with grains and fruits.

This fully-opened cone shows the spiked bracts.

Unopened cones contain the edible pine seeds.

Pine tree

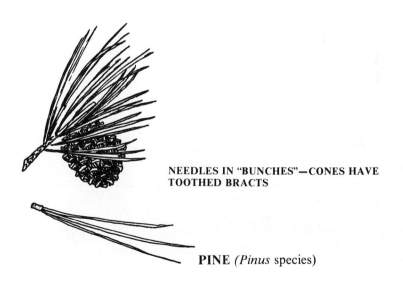

**NEEDLES IN "BUNCHES"—CONES HAVE
TOOTHED BRACTS**

PINE *(Pinus* species)

INDIAN PLUM *(Osmaronia cerasiformis)*

The wild plum, more correctly known as Indian plum, has a long history of use by early natives and was widely used by settlers. It became particularly popular in western Canada, where preserves were once commercially prepared and shipped to eastern markets.

Indian plum seems to be more influenced by conditions during the growing season than any other wild fruit. One year a tree may bear a few tiny plums, while the same tree a season later will bear the weight of hundreds of plump fruits. The season in which this was written was an especially productive one, with many trees holding huge masses of fruit.

Habitat and distribution: Indian plum prefers the more moist ground of the lower elevations and is seldom found in dry or rocky ground. It grows in dense thickets, often along stream banks and roadways. It is limited to the western side of the Cascades and Sierras from California to upper British Columbia and southeast Alaska.

Description: Indian plum is among the earliest spring plants to begin budding; the flowers appear in April or May. The fruits often form late in May if the season has been mild. The leaves are fairly long and tapered, being well veined and random along the stem. They are darker above and slightly hairy beneath.

The fruits of Indian plum hang in clusters.

INDIAN PLUM *(Osmaronia cerasiformis)*

**SPRING BLOOMS OF MANY WHITE
"STAR" FLOWERS**

The fruits hang in clusters below the stem, following masses of white star-shaped flowers. The fruits are yellow at first, blushing with red, then becoming a dark bluish-black with a blue powdery bloom on the skins.

Use: You can pick three or four gallons of Indian plums in an hour during good seasons. They are not overly flavorful and the seeds are large, but they provide good eating nonetheless. If you are collecting Indian plums for the cooking pot, take most of the fruits from the tree, even those that are obviously not quite ripe. The greener fruit seems to have a greater amount of pectin, and the addition of a small percentage makes a better jelly without substantially affecting the flavor.

Dry the plums for storage or future use, then soak them in water for a few hours and use as a fresh plum. A few pitted fruits make an excellent addition to a dry cereal product. Traveling parties of Indians often carried the sun-dried fruits because they were light and tasty and did not spoil on the trail.

RASPBERRY *(Rubus* species)

The wild red raspberry should be familiar to anyone who has ever picked or eaten domestic raspberries. There is essentially no difference between the two in either appearance or flavor. (A close relative, the black raspberry, is considered separately since identification is different.)

The red raspberry played an important part in the diet of the far northern Indian tribes. It was highly regarded by those tribes farther south but was less critical because of the abundance of other fruits.

Although the table shows a vitamin C content of about 18 milligrams, let me quote from the University of Alaska Extension Service publication #28 ("Wild Edible and Poisonous Plants of Alaska, 1974"): "The berries can be used in much the same way as strawberries, raw with sugar and cream, as berry shortcake, pie. The fresh berry is a very rich source of vitamin C, the antiscorbutic vitamin. When frozen immediately after picking and kept frozen until ready for use, the berry retains much of its vitamin C value. One sample of berries kept in an ice cellar from collecting time in the fall until April of the following year was found to contain 178 milligrams ascorbic acid per 100 grams." That's quite a variation from the 18 milligrams claimed by the USDA for more southerly berries.

Habitat and distribution: Red raspberry has an incredibly wide range, from the dry slopes of the Rockies into south-central Alaska. With the possible exception of blue huckleberry, it is probably the most abundant wild fruit in the central parts of Alaska and northern Canada. (In those areas, cranberry is more widespread, but is not found in such large numbers.) Red raspberry generally prefers dry soils, but is found flourishing in the acid grounds of the far north, ranging as far as the Yukon and central Alaska. It grows in open ground or in scattered openings in the forests. It appears in abundance in cutover lands with fireweed and salal.

Description: Red raspberry has a stout stem from which several thinner stems branch. The leaves are compound with three to five leaflets each. Each is pointed with pronounced teeth and veins and often has a powdery bloom. The stalk displays short, weak spines and a bluish bloom. The red berries are composed of many drupelets and are supported by short, erect sepals. As with all raspberries, the pithy core remains on the plant when the berry is picked.

Use: Collect red raspberries easily from head-high bushes; they are delicious raw. Their best use in the field is with a little milk and sugar added.

At home, the berries make excellent jams and jellies. There is no difference in the use of these and commercial species, except that you collect them yourself.

Depending on conditions, red raspberry may vary from a scrubby bush as shown here, to a long, trailing stem.

Looking exactly like cultivated raspberries, the wild fruit is red and has small seeds throughout. Note the raspberry.

NEEDLE-LIKE SPINES

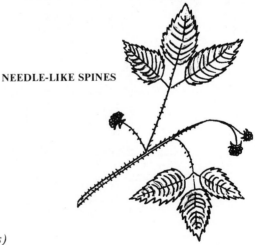

RASPBERRY *(Rubus idaeus)*

281

RASPBERRY, BLACKCAP *(Rubus* species)

The blackcap or black raspberry is similar to the red raspberry in general appearance, but it has a unique tartness. Words fail to adequately communicate the subtle differences between this and any other taste. The historical uses of black raspberry are essentially the same as of the red, but smaller range limits the amount of previous use.

Habitat and distribution: Black raspberries choose the moister climates of the west slopes of the Cascade range, but are often found in drier ground within this zone. They are prolific in the thousands of acres of logged-off grounds in the western part of the coastal states and Canada.

Description: Black raspberry usually grows as a gracefully arching plant that is quite vinelike, with only small branches leaving the heavy main stalk. The thorns are strong, sharp, and recurved. The compound leaves are pale green above and flashing silver beneath; they are very similar to red raspberries, but the silver underside differentiates them. The older plants have a definitely purple stalk.

The shallow, flattened berry is black or very dark blue, with stiff sepals supporting it. The berry has pronounced bristly hairs protruding from each drupelet.

Use: These berries are nutritionally about the same as red raspberries. Use them the same as the red raspberry, but watch the thorns. They are tough and sharp!

One kind of black raspberry grows on graceful, bending stalks.

Blackcap. Note the sharp thorns.

BRISTLY BLACK BERRIES

**LEAVES "SILVERY" BENEATH SHARP,
CURVED SPINES**

BLACK RASPBERRY *(Rubus leucodermis)*

283

ROSE *(Rosa* species)

The wild roses—there are more than a hundred species—are found in almost any environment. Only an expert could differentiate even half of them. The differences are unimportant to us, since all bear edible fruit and flowers.

Roses have a long history of medicinal uses and superstitious applications, but were also quite widely used as foods. Like the raspberry, they were historically collected in Alaska for food by the early natives, and the miners and settlers who followed kept the tradition alive.

Across America, the Indians prepared an almost universal confection by candying the cooked fruit (called rosehip). They boiled it lightly in thickened sap from the maple or sugar pines, after which it was stored with minimum risk.

The jams and jellies of rosehips were popular in turn-of-the-century America but seemed to fall from popularity after the establishment of large commercial berry plantations. It's a shame, for none of the berries duplicate the tart goodness of the rosehip. Rosehips are a valuable wild edible. A neighbor of mine in Alaska used to make at least five gallons of jelly a year. She claimed it kept her burgeoning brood from having so many colds. Whether it did the trick or not is quite unprovable, but something sure did. Her ten kids were healthy, happy, completely unaffected by modern education, and a joy to know!

Habitat and distribution: Because of the many species and their tested adaptability, we can safely say that wild rose is found throughout the continent.

Description: The familiar roses are characterized by thorny, bushy thickets and numerous flowers, mostly pink, but sometimes varying from white to red. The leaves are typical of cultivated roses, being in compound leaves of an uneven number of leaflets, usually ranging from five to nine. The leafy flowers become the fruits, or hips, which are scarlet, red, or a bright orange. The pulpy hips may hang on the bush long after the leaves have fallen and are a winter source of food in most places.

Use: You can collect the fruits easily and eat them raw or cooked. The pulpier hips make the best jam or jelly, but all are good. Many people discard the seeds, but they contain a lot of vitamin E. Grind them, boil them, and strain through cheesecloth. Substitute the resulting syrup for any breakfast syrup.

Steep the flower petals into a delicious, aromatic tea, or put them in salads for a delightfully different flavor. Boil and crush a pot of rosehips, then allow it to jell and cool to provide an excellent side sauce for a pot roast or spit-roasted wild fowl.

Wild rose

Rosehip

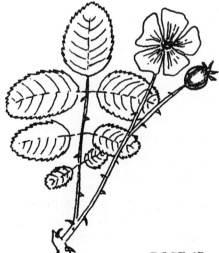

ROSE *(Rosa* species) *color photo, page 171*

SALAL *(Gaultheria* species)

The two species of salal are easily the most widespread forest shrub. Salal was very important to the early Indians and is one of the few plants to retain its native name. The Indians dried the mealy berries for use in pemmican, and the dried cakes became an important source of trade. Salal is prevalent along the windswept coastal cliffs and into the upper mountains.

Because of the difficult conditions where it is found, salal has developed into a tough, flexible plant that can lie flattened under heavy snows for weeks, then spring back into an upright position with no injury. Foul weather and snow don't damage the thick leathery leaves.

Habitat and distribution: One of the two species is largely limited to the bank of moist ground west of the Cascades in California, Oregon, and Washington, and east Idaho. In British Columbia it is quite abundant nearly the full breadth of the province. It prefers moist, shady habitats. The other one goes from the coast to the western slope of the Cascades and coastal ranges, British Columbia to southern California.

Description: Salal is a low shrubby evergreen that often forms a knee-deep cover over the forest floor. In some parts of the Northwest, it makes an impenetrable mass up to 10 feet deep that requires heavy machetes just to pass through. The stems are flexible and quite strong, as are the larger stalks and

Salal

286

SALAL *(Gaultheria shallon)*

(color photo, page 175)

limbs. The leaves are egg-shaped, nearly entire or finely toothed, tough, and leathery. They are deep glossy green above and whiter beneath. The flowers, which bloom from early spring to mid-summer, are borne in stubby racemes. One key to the identification of this plant is a prominent bract and two bractlets at the base of the flower stem or peduncle.

The urn-shaped flowers are white or pink. The fruits are of similar shape, thick-skinned, mealy, and nearly black. They remain on the branches well into the fall, giving the forager a period of many weeks to collect and enjoy the fresh berries.

Use: You can collect the fruits easily from the unarmed bushes and eat them raw but they are somewhat better after cooking. The berries are not very juicy, but you can make a good fruit cider quickly by crushing and boiling them, extracting as much juice as possible. To this, add an equal amount of water and allow to cool. (If you cap it tightly and allow it to ferment in the bottle, it makes a rather effective form of fruity beer.)

Strain and further boil the juice from the berries to make an outstanding syrup.

SALMONBERRY *(Rubus spectabilis)*

The common salmonberry is an excellent golden berry that has, for some reason, gained a reputation for being inedible.

The berry found wide acceptance by the Indians, who usually ate it raw over a biscuit of rough flour. It may have been the forerunner of our modern shortcake dishes. (Incidentally, salmonberries over shortcake with a dash of sweet cream or whipped cream makes an especially delightful dessert.)

The berries of salmonberry aren't very nutritious and closely parallel the regular raspberries in that respect.

Habitat and distribution: Salmonberries prefer cool, moist conditions and usually crowd the shores of streams and small creeks. They are plentiful along the shores of wooded lakes and thrive in any cool situation. They are generally limited to the wet coastal zones but may occur in other places along the northern portion.

Description: Salmonberries are large rounded bushes. The drooping outer stems bear the majority of the leaves and all the flowers and fruits. The

Salmonberries

288

SALMONBERRY *(Rubus spectabilis)*

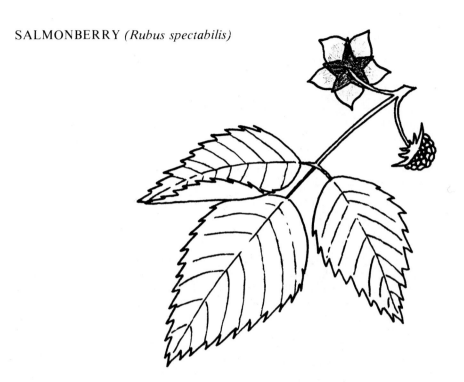

(color photo, page 175)

leaves are compound, almost always in threes, and closely resemble the raspberries in shape and size. The flowers are a delicate red; they are seen for as long as three months, beginning in April.

As with other members of this family, the berries are composed of many drupelets and leave their pithy core on the bush when picked. The fruits are similar to raspberries but range in color from golden yellow to a translucent reddish-gold. The berries are fairly large, more elongated than the raspberry, and the taste is in no way similar. You must experience it to understand.

Use: You can pick salmonberries from the lightly armed bushes with relative ease. Eat them raw or cook them into fine jams, clear jellies, or a good filling for pies. You can make a sweet wine from them that rivals many commercial wines in flavor.

SERVICEBERRY *(Amelanchier* species)

The several species of this bush provide clouds of white blossoms in early spring and an almost endless supply of small berries in late spring and summer.

The small berries are not widely used any longer but were once a staple fruit. Early Indians and settlers found many uses for serviceberry. Regionally known as "sarviceberry," it was the most popular berry for making pemmican. It was made into large dried cakes and transported along the trails of the nomadic tribes of the central plains. The cakes could be soaked in water, after which they regained most of their fresh weight and flavor. The dried fruits were often added to soups and stews.

Habitat and distribution: Serviceberry is widespread and abundant throughout North America. West of the Cascades it is limited to elevations below about 2000 feet. It becomes less common in the northern limits of its range, but is prolific in the drier interior regions.

Description: Serviceberry is a large deciduous shrub, possibly reaching 15 feet in height, but more often from 6 to 12 feet. It is an open, spreading shrub with many leaves. Foragers often overlook it because it is usually mixed in with other bushes and tends to grow in thick clusters.

The simple leaves are petioled and have teeth on only the outer half, although older leaves may develop teeth well down the margins. The young leaves are toothed only along the extreme outer end.

White serviceberry blossoms almost cover the bushes in April and May, giving way to large numbers of small seedy berries later in the season. The berries are from red to black, usually showing a trace of the petals at the bottom of the fruit.

Clusters of serviceberries.

Use: Take some care in picking these berries because they sometimes become pretty wormy. The birds and animals aren't too fussy about that, but you might be. If a tree is wormy, chances are all the fruits are affected, but other nearby trees may be completely free of the pests and you can collect the berries without much difficulty. Eat them raw or cooked. They make excellent jams, although they are a bit seedy. As a jelly fruit they are superb. Serviceberry pies taste a lot like huckleberry pies, but lack the characteristic tartness of the huckleberries. They also make into fruit cider or wines.

Under emergency conditions, dry the berries into cakes to carry along. To use, soak them in water until they soften.

White blossoms cover this serviceberry bush.

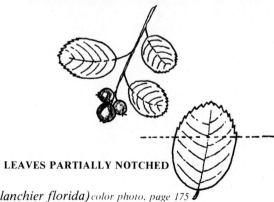

LEAVES PARTIALLY NOTCHED

SERVICEBERRY *(Amelanchier florida) color photo, page 175*

STRAWBERRY *(Fragaria* species)

Wild strawberries are perhaps the most awaited of all the early summer berries. They are just as popular with birds, especially robins, as with humans, and the competition is intense. You have to find a patch that the birds haven't taken, but that usually isn't too difficult.

Just as popular with the Indians as the fruit of this fine plant was an aromatic tea brewed from its leaves. It is still incorporated in some of the so-called gourmet teas that are available in specialty shops across the country.

Habitat and distribution: Wild strawberry prefers sunny slopes or openings in the forest canopy. It adapts well to either moist or dry climates and is found virtually anywhere except the Arctic or desert regions.

Description: Wild strawberry is very similar to the cultivated plants except for size; it is smaller with much smaller fruits.

The leaves are erect, composed of three leaflets. They are oval, well toothed, and supported on long, viny stems.

The flowers are typical strawberry blossoms, five white petals with a green bract beneath each. The leaves, flowers, and runners all connect directly with the roots. The runners are a key to the identification of the plant. They spread some distance away, develop a new root, and support two or three sets of leaflets that are perfect miniatures of the adult leaves.

The scarlet berries are a single pulpy mass with the many fruits adhering to the receptable. They are scale models of the cultivated berries, but smaller in size and richer in flavor.

Use: Although they are small and tedious to collect, the flavor of these tiny berries is unrivaled by anything the commercial field can offer and worth the time it takes to find and pick them. They are best when eaten raw. There is no wilderness treat that can compare with a bowl of fresh wild strawberries topped with a dash of cold milk or cream. Although the berry makes an outstanding jelly, it is much more valuable as a jam, since the pulp of the berry retains the sweet flavor just as well as the juices.

A wild strawberry pie on a flaky graham crust topped with whipped cream is probably the ultimate dessert. Because of the difficulty of collecting the berries in large numbers, this pie is never available commercially. It is a special delight reserved for those who gather the fruit for themselves.

Whenever you are out picking strawberries, collect a handful of the mature leaves. Allow them to dry at home, then crush them as a fine tea or an addition to other natural teas you have collected.

Wild strawberry in bloom.

WILD STRAWBERRY *(Fragaria cuneifolia)*

THIMBLEBERRY *(Rubus parviflorus)*

Thimbleberry is something of an anomaly among the many members of this genus. While it is closely related to the raspberries, salmonberry, and blackberries, it does not share their three-leaflet characteristic. The flavor of thimbleberry is also a wide departure from that of the other members of its clan.

The early natives utilized virtually all the fruits and plants that appeared, simply as a matter of survival. Although they probably didn't think a great deal of this particular plant, they did collect and eat it in substantial numbers. Usually they cooked the berries into a sauce or a sort of jam and ate them with other foods. They were abundant in most areas, and good advantage was taken of their availability.

Habitat and distribution: Thimbleberry is abundant to the point of being a pest in damp, shady situations. It is especially prevalent along stream banks and ditch lines. It is found in any suitable habitat but is especially easy to find in the northern part. It ranges well into Canada and southeast Alaska.

Description: Thimbleberry may grow to four or five feet but is often only two feet high in drier climates. It is best recognized by the characteristic

Thimbleberry

294

maple-shaped leaves that appear in a flat umbel near the top of the plant and are spread all around the short branches. The leaves are deeply lobed and have a soft, porous texture.

The plant produces many large white blossoms in the spring. They are usually five-petaled and have large sepals behind each petal.

The berries are flattened, somewhat resembling a raspberry. They are an extremely bright red color, somewhat flat in taste, and not very popular.

Use: You can eat thimbleberries raw, but the flavor is not very good and some people find them somewhat distasteful.

As a basis for jam, they are fine, but add another fruit to them for the added pectin and change in flavor. Gooseberries or crab apples are often added to the mass in the cooking kettle to improve the final product.

TWINBERRY *(Lonicera involucrata)*

This member of the honeysuckle family grows abundantly and provides an excellent fruit. Although twinberry was probably as widely used by the early residents of this country as the orange honeysuckle, there are few records of any of the Indian tribes collecting it in numbers. The early records come from the journals of pioneers and homesteaders, who made a fine wine and excellent preserves from it.

It was popular as an occasional dessert, eaten raw or baked into pies and rolls. Many of the Scandinavian fishermen who first came to the Northwest made good use of twinberry in traditional baked desserts.

Habitat and distribution: Twinberry is generally found in moist thickets. It prefers stream banks and the margins of small lakes and ponds, in particular those associated with coniferous forests.

Description: Twinberry is an erect bushy shrub. It is almost impossible to mistake for any other plant because of the unique twin arrangement of flowers and fruits on the stems. The leaves are lanceolate to egg-shaped, opposite, and quite tapering.

A pair of small yellow flowers is borne on each short pedicel growing from the opposite leaf axils. Each pair is cupped with green bracts that become reddish or dark red as the fruit matures. The fruits occupy the same relative positions and the twin berries are black.

Use: Enjoy twinberry for its delightful flavor and many fine uses. Raw, the small black berries are quite pleasant. Make them into pies and other sweet fillings or use them for jams, jellies, or wines. Cook the berries into a quick sauce, allow it to jell, and serve as a side to meats during a stay in a fishing camp or other outdoor activity.

BLACK TWINBERRY *(Lonicera involucrata)*

CHAPTER 4
Using Wild Grains

As more people become interested in the fun of foraging and the healthful aspects of using the wild edibles, it is natural that they begin to think of making their own flour. Home made or stone-ground flours are becoming popular—and expensive because of the increased demand.

Earlier in this book, I discussed a great many seeds and pollens that can be ground into flour, as well as several root plants that can be cooked into a mush, dried, and then reduced to a fine flour. Unfortunately, these products seldom provide the essential nutrients of the grain-based flours, particularly the plant protein and the B vitamins that are so critical to the maintenance of good health.

Commercially prepared flours are easy to use and plentiful, but they too are becoming more costly. More important, the bleaching and milling processes that are currently used reduce the amount of nutrient that is finally baked into your products at home. Just how dramatic these losses are is best illustrated by the following figures, comparing the value of the whole grain with an unenriched commercial (patent) flour.

| | In Milligrams | | |
	Thiamine	Riboflavin	Niacin
Wheat	0.57	0.12	4.3
Patent flour	.06	.05	.9

Of course, agents are normally added to the flours to make them salable as "enriched" products that have essentially regained the value of the whole wheat. Unfortunately, these are often synthetic vitamins or other additives that are contrary to the healthy reasons for wanting to use the whole grain products in the first place.

This is not a criticism of the commercial milling industry, which has an almost impossible job keeping up with massive demand. On a small scale, though, you can easily make a superior product in your own kitchen if you care to go to the work of making stone-ground flours.

Making your own flour isn't the mysterious process most people seem to think. There are only three steps: threshing, parching, and grinding. Here, we'll consider only the simplest techniques, those that worked quite satisfactorily for many households in the past. They are also still seen working in many of the underdeveloped parts of the world.

First, consider the raw material. It is possible, of course, to list many wild grains here and make comments about each. Fortunately, that is unnecessary.

All of the wild grains in this country will do nicely for the production of stone-ground flours. To the best of my knowledge, most of the common grasses or grains are not harmful to humans, provided the threshing, parching, and grinding are done sufficiently.

Threshing is the process of removing the grain heads from the stems, usually known as straws. The simplest method is to strip the heads off by hand, which is very effective for gathering small quantities. You need a bucket or basket to collect grain in larger quantities. The most effective method is to gather large handfuls of the grasses, bend them over the edge of your basket, and beat them with your hand or a stout stick. This is particularly effective if the grains are well ripened (and collect only ripe grains).

Then transfer the grains to a large shallow container such as an old-fashioned threshing basket or a large dishpan and allow them to dry in the sun.

Wild oats can be easily collected by stripping the stalks upward.

Winnowing the grain.

After they are well dried, they can be further threshed and cleaned by throwing them into the air and catching them in the basket. The very light husk blows away, and the clean grains fall straight back down into the basket. This method does not remove all the husks, but certainly helps get them much cleaner.

Parching is a quick roasting process that is more important for removing the remaining husks and beards than for any cooking of the heart of the kernel that may occur. If the grain is thoroughly dried in the sun, no cooking is required, but the open-flame parching does get rid of the barbed hairs and coverings.

Parching is best accomplished, at least in my experience, in a screen carrier of some kind, in which a very thin layer of grain is done all at one time. A flat-bottomed screen strainer works well in the field, or you may wish to manufacture some kind of screen of your own.

Pass the thin layer of grain over an open flame several times, but don't leave it in the fire long enough to burn the grain. This is not hard to do, and you'll see the bright flashes of the husks burning without singeing the hearts of the grain. After parching, the grain is firm and smooth to the touch and has only the shiny kernels remaining. At this stage, it is ready to grind into a rough flour.

Grinding between two large porous stones is the best method of making a flour of your cleaned and parched grain. This process has been used for many centuries to make flour, cracked cereal, and meal. What product you end up with depends entirely on how much elbow grease you put into the grinding operation.

The two-stone method was used by primitive peoples down through history, and the early mills didn't change it much, although the stones were much larger and moved by wind or water power. Today's mills, powered by huge electric motors, still use the same techniques, but more modern abrasive devices that can turn out huge quantities of flour in a short time have replaced the stones.

The old method of grinding flour.

Ideally, the bottom stone is slightly concave to hold the grain in place while it is ground. The upper stone is cylindrical to provide good handholds and plenty of grinding surface below. You may want to put the lower stone in a frame, or at least on a large plastic or canvas sheet, so the grain and flour are easily collected after you have ground it. Every few minutes, scoop up the grain that has come off the grindstone and return it until your flour is as fine as you want it. More pressure on the stone and more grinding steps produce a finer and finer flour. It is not necessary to reach the powdery stage of the commercial flours. Your flour will almost always be brownish because it is not bleached, producing cakes and biscuits of a standard whole wheat or cracked wheat color.

These primitive steps easily produce a fine nutritious flour that you can use in any baking you choose. Soon, commercial flours and bakery breads just won't be good enough any longer.

During the grinding process, set a good portion aside after it has just been cracked and rolled into a coarse meal. Roast this for a while and add some chopped nuts and fresh fruit. With milk and sugar, you'll have a delicious, healthful breakfast cereal, and you will be following a morning tradition that has lasted for thousands of years, disappearing only in the recent age of mass production, artificial nutrients, and TV commercials. It's kind of fun to have a fine cereal, knowing you need not depend on the breakfast-food hucksters for such a product.

Incidentally, the large food manufacturers are finally beginning to make these natural cereals that take fewer steps and less sophisticated methods. In fact, they are quite like those you can make for yourself. As you might have expected, these "new" cereal products are much more expensive than the conventional types.

It is doubtful that many of us will ever grind all our own flour, but the knowledge is comforting. If you go on an extended camping trip, it might be fun to spend a morning collecting grains, threshing and drying them, and removing the husk. The grinding process, a day or two later after the grains are well dried, may result in the coarsest of flours, but the hotcakes and biscuits you make will be all the better for the work you have put into them. And you'll know that there really isn't much mystery in the whole process. o

Rough ground flour is returned to the stone to produce a finer flour.

POISONOUS PLANTS

The one drawback to foraging is the possibility of collecting plants that are potentially dangerous. Here and there among the wild edibles outlined in this book, I've pointed out the parts or conditions that rendered some poisonous. The plants listed here are extremely dangerous. Never collect them under any circumstances.

The only practical way to avoid the difficulties of dangerous plants is to collect and eat only those you know are edible, those that you can positively identify as safe. Experimenting with unknown or unfamiliar wild growth may jeopardize your health or your very life.

Because there are so many harmful plants west of the Rockies, it is impossible to list them all here. In fact, the toxic effects of many plants is still not completely known and it would be impossible to talk about them with any authority. Instead, I will try to list the most common poisonous plants and those that have a significant history of causing poisoning in humans.

Since most house plants and garden ornamentals are dangerous, it is best to assume that *all* of them are inedible, unless you can positively identify one as being an edible variety. Some of these plants are among the deadliest in the entire plant kingdom.

Some wild plants contain very potent toxins. The water hemlock *(Cicuta maculata)* and two closely related plants, water parsnip *(Sium suave)* and poison hemlock *(Conium maculatum),* are the most dangerous of all wild plants in North America. They are best identified by an unusual leaf structure, in which the veins run to the notches of the dentate leaflets, rather than to the points of the teeth. Poison hemlock leaves are finely divided, almost fernlike. All three plants usually show mottled purple colors on stems and leaves, are aromatic, and have very definite sheaths where each branch leaves the main stem. Poison hemlock is locally abundant in dry or waste ground, while the other two are found in or near water and are less widely distributed.

This deadly trio is probably responsible for more deaths in humans and livestock than any other. They are quick-acting and almost always debilitating or fatal; there is no known chemical antidote for the poisons. Only symptomatic treatment can be applied, and it is often unsuccessful. It is essential that the collector of wild plants know these plants well.

High on the list of plants causing human death is the thorn apple or jimson weed. This plant seems to appeal particularly to children, who seldom survive the strong toxins contained throughout.

The following list of plants contains the majority of the most often encountered poisons. If you want information on the poisonous plants, consult a good text on the subject that has been assembled specifically for the area in which you forage. Above all, DON'T EAT ANY PLANT UNLESS YOU ARE POSITIVE IT IS SAFE!

POISON HEMLOCK *(Conium maculatum)*

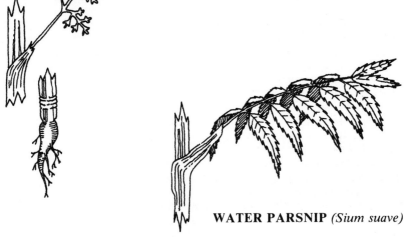

WATER PARSNIP *(Sium suave)*

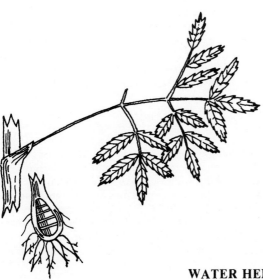

WATER HEMLOCK *(Cicuta maculata)*

COMMON TOXIC PLANTS

Name of plant	*Toxic portion*
Azalea *(Rhododendron occidentale)*	Leaves, may be fatal
Baneberry *(Actaea arguta)*	Berries, may be fatal
Bleeding heart *(Dicentra formosa)*	All parts, causes severe gastric problems
Buttercup *(Ranunculus acris, R. repens)*	All parts, intense burning of mouth and lips
Cherry *(Prunus emarginata* and others*)*	Leaves, may be fatal to children
Death camas *(Zygadenus venenosus)*	Bulbs, fatal if eaten in any quantity
Delphinium *(Delphinium occidentale)*	Leaves, may be fatal
Foxglove *(Digitalis purpurea)*	All parts, powerful heart stimulant, may be fatal
Iris *(Iris tenax and others)*	Underground parts, may be fatal
Ivy *(Glechoma hederacea)*	Leaves, not usually fatal, but very serious
Jimson weed *(Datura stramonium)*	All parts, quite often fatal
Larkspur *(Delphinium menziesii)*	Leaves, often fatal
Lily of the valley *(Maianthemum unifolium dilatatum)*	All parts, may be fatal
Lobelia *(Lobelia dortmanna* and others*)*	All parts, may be fatal
Lupine *(Lupinus pusillus* and others*)*	Seeds, not usually fatal, but may cause permanent physical and nervous damage
Nightshade *(Solanum nigrum* and others*)*	Berries, usually fatal
Poison hemlock *(Conium maculatum)*	All parts, usually fatal
Red elderberry *(Sambucus callicarpa)*	Berries, not usually fatal
Rhododendron *(Rhododendron macrophyllum)*	Leaves and flowers, has been fatal
Spreading dogbane *(Apocynum cannabinum)*	All parts, may be fatal
Sweet pea *(Lathyrus latifolius and others)*	Seeds and stems, not usually fatal, but serious
Tansy ragwort *(Senecio jocobaea)*	Leaves, have proven fatal to cattle
Vetch *(Vicia angustifolia)*	Seeds, some varieties dangerous but seldom fatal
Water hemlock *(Cicuta maculata)*	All parts, usually fatal
Water parsnip *(Sium suave)*	All parts, usually fatal
Yew *(Taxus brevifolia)*	All parts, death may occur after ingestion with no warning or prior symptoms

Obviously, these plants are much more dangerous to small children than to adults, who probably won't try them anyway. Kids usually need much less toxin than adults to prove harmful, because toxic doses are generally measured in percentages of body weight. When you forage with the family, it is essential that you teach them the key rule: don't eat anything unless you are certain it is safe.

NUTRITION TABLE

Plant	Food Energy Cal.	Protein Gm	Fat Gm	Carbohydrate Total	Carbohydrate Fiber	Calcium Mg	Phosphorus Mg	Iron Mg	Sodium Mg	Potassium Mg	Vitamin A I.U.	Thiamine Mg	Riboflavin Mg	Niacin Mg	Ascorbic Acid Mg
Balsamroot, seed	560	24.0	47.3	19.9	3.8	120	837	7.1	30	920	50	1.96	.23	5.4	—
Camas lily	113	0.7	.23	27.1	1.3	—	—	—	—	—	—	.07	.05	—	4
Carrot	42	1.1	.2	9.7	1.0	37	36	.7	47	341	—	.06	.05	.6	8
Dandelion greens, *raw*	45	2.7	.7	9.2	1.6	187	66	3.1	76	397	14,000	.19	.26	—	35
cooked	33	2.0	.6	6.4	1.3	140	42	1.8	44	232	11,700	.13	.16	—	18
Dock *raw*	28	2.1	.3	5.6	.8	66	41	1.6	5	338	12,900	.09	.22	.5	119
cooked	19	1.6	.2	3.9	.7	55	26	.9	3	198	10,800	.06	.13	.4	54
Goatsbeard *raw*	*	2.9	.6	18.0	1.8	47	66	1.5	—	380	10	.04	.04	.3	11
cooked	*	2.6	.6	15.1	1.8	42	53	1.3	—	266	10	.03	.04	.2	7
Lamb's quarters *raw*	43	4.2	.8	7.3	2.1	309	72	1.2	—	—	11,600	.16	.44	1.2	80
cooked	32	3.2	.7	5.0	1.8	258	45	.7	—	—	9,700	.10	.26	.9	37
Leek	52	2.2	.3	11.2	1.3	52	50	1.1	5	347	40	.11	.06	.5	17
Mustard *raw*	31	3.0	.5	5.6	1.1	183	50	3.0	32	377	7,000	.11	.22	.8	97
cooked	23	2.2	.4	4.0	.9	138	32	1.8	18	220	5,800	.08	.14	.6	48
Onion (bulb and entire top)	36	1.5	.2	8.2	1.2	51	39	1.0	5	231	2,000	.05	.05	.4	32
Pigweed	36	3.5	.5	6.5	1.3	267	67	3.9	—	411	6,100	.08	.16	1.4	80
Sheep sorrel	28	2.1	.3	5.6	.8	66	41	1.6	5	338	12,900	.09	.22	.5	119
Watercress	19	2.2	.3	3.0	.7	151	54	1.7	52	282	4,900	.08	.16	.9	79
Raspberry, black	73	1.5	1.4	15.7	5.1	30	22	.9	1	199	Trace	.03	.09	.9	18
Cranberry	46	.4	.7	10.8	1.4	14	10	.5	2	82	40	.03	.02	.1	11
Elderberry	72	2.6	.5	16.4	7.0	38	28	1.6	—	300	600	.07	.06	.5	36
Hazelnut	634	12.6	62.4	16.7	3.0	209	337	3.4	2	704	—	.46	—	.9	Trace
Oregon crab apple	68	.4	.3	17.8	.6	6	13	.3	1	110	40	.03	.02	.1	8
Raspberry, red	57	1.2	.5	13.6	3.0	22	22	.9	1	168	130	.03	.09	.9	25
Rosehips	56	.6	.3	14.2	1.1	29	16	1.2	—	—	130	.02	.03	.8	22
Strawberry	37	.7	.5	8.4	1.3	21	21	1.0	1	164	60	.03	.07	.6	59
Currant (red and white)	50	1.4	.2	12.1	3.4	32	23	1.0	2	257	120	.04	.05	.1	41

Watt, B. K. and Merrill, A. L. *Composition of Foods.* USDA Agriculture Handbook No. 8.

Table based on cultivated plants so values cannot be taken as absolute.

—Values range from 13 calories fresh to 82 calories after storage.

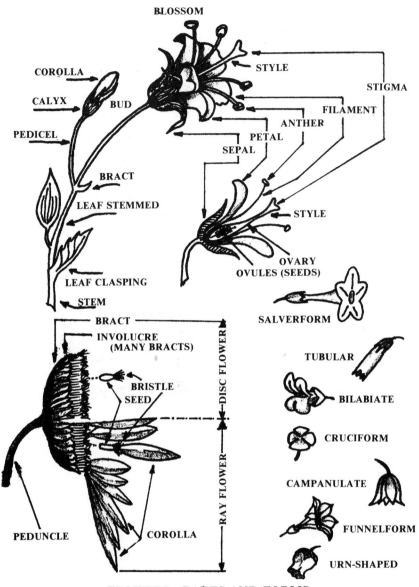

BLOSSOM

COROLLA

CALYX

BUD

PEDICEL

STYLE

STIGMA

FILAMENT

ANTHER

PETAL

SEPAL

STYLE

BRACT

LEAF STEMMED

OVARY
OVULES (SEEDS)

LEAF CLASPING

STEM

SALVERFORM

BRACT

INVOLUCRE
(MANY BRACTS)

DISC FLOWER

TUBULAR

BRISTLE
SEED

BILABIATE

CRUCIFORM

RAY FLOWER

CAMPANULATE

PEDUNCLE

COROLLA

FUNNELFORM

URN-SHAPED

FLOWERS—PARTS AND FORMS

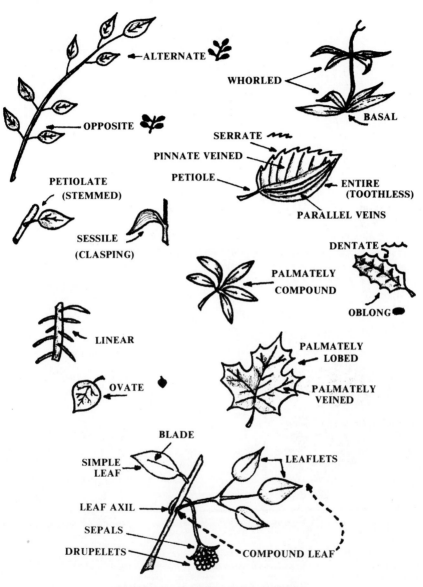

ALTERNATE

WHORLED

BASAL

OPPOSITE

SERRATE

PINNATE VEINED

PETIOLE

ENTIRE
(TOOTHLESS)

PETIOLATE
(STEMMED)

PARALLEL VEINS

SESSILE
(CLASPING)

DENTATE

PALMATELY
COMPOUND

OBLONG

LINEAR

PALMATELY
LOBED

OVATE

PALMATELY
VEINED

BLADE

SIMPLE
LEAF

LEAFLETS

LEAF AXIL

SEPALS

DRUPELETS

COMPOUND LEAF

LEAVES—PARTS AND FORMS

GLOSSARY

Acute—*sharp-pointed, but not long-tapered*

Alternate—*only one leaf at a node, followed by another leaf on the other side of the stem*

Annual—*a plant that completes its life-cycle and dies in one growing season*

Apex—*the point farthest from the base or point of attachment*

Appendage—*any special outgrowth or prolongation of a structure*

Axil—*the angle between a leaf and a stem*

Basal—*from the base of the plant*

Beaked—*tipped with a point*

Berry—*a pulpy or juicy, several or many-seeded fruit*

Biennial—*a plant that completes its life-cycle and dies in two growing seasons*

Blade—*the usually flat expanded part of a leaf*

Bloom—*fine, powdery deposit on the surface of a fruit or leaf*

Bract—*modified or reduced leaf in a flower or flower cluster*

Bulb—*thickened underground stem base as of a lily or onion*

Calyx—*lowest (outermost) part of the flower, usually not colorful*

Capsule—*dry, compound fruit that splits at maturity; a pod*

Cleft—*cut about to the middle*

Compound—*made up of two or more parts, as with some leaves*

Deciduous—*falling after maturity, as leaves fall at the end of the growing season*

Dentate—*toothed*

Disk flower—*tubular flower in members of the sunflower family*

Divided—*in leaves, having the segments of the blade distinctly separated from each other on the main stem*

Drupe—*pulpy, usually one-seeded fruit, such as a cherry, with a fleshy outer part enclosing a stone that contains the seed*

Drupelet—*tiny drupe, such as the divisions of a blackberry*

Entire—*not cut or toothed*

Evergreen—*green throughout the year*

Fruit—*ripened ovary along with any other parts developing with it; the part of the plant that contains the seed*

Gland—*usually a small organ that secretes oil or nectar*

Habitat—*environment in which a plant typically grows*

Head—*compact cluster of flowers, such as the dandelion*

Herb—*plant whose stem above ground is not woody and dies at the end of the season's growth*

Hoary—*gray from a minute hairy covering*

Incised—*of leaves, having margins sharply and deeply notched*

Lanceolate—*lance-shaped*

Lateral—*at the side*

312

Leaflet—*leaflike division of a compound leaf*
Limb—*blade of a petal or leaf*
Linear—*very narrow with nearly parallel sides*
Lobe—*shallow division of a leaf or other organ*
Node—*point of attachment of leaf to stem*
Oblong—*leaf form in which the length is considerably greater than the width with the sides nearly parallel*
Obtuse—*rounded*
Opposite—*of leaves, two at a node, on either side of a stem*
Palmate—*radiating out from a central point like the fingers of the hand*
Peduncle—*stalk of a flower cluster or of a single flower when solitary*
Perennial—*plant that lives and fruits for an indefinite number of years, but more than two*
Perfoliate—*opposite leaves joined at the base through which the stem appears to pass*
Persistent—*remaining attached after maturity*
Petal—*part of the flower, usually colorful*
Petiole—*leaf stalk*
Pinnate—*evenly distributed along the sides of a common axis, like a feather*
Pistil—*seed-bearing organ of a flower, consisting of ovary, style, and stigma*
Pollen—*powdery grains borne on the anthers of the stamen*
Prostrate—*lying flat on the ground*
Pungent—*prickly-pointed; sharp-tasting*
Raceme—*flower cluster in which the flowers are borne on stems of nearly uniform length, arranged on the sides of the same peduncle*
Regular—*with all the petals or sepals of a flower alike*
Reticulate—*forming a network pattern*
Rhizome—*underground, rootlike stem*
Rootstock—*Rootlike underground stem*
Rosette—*circular cluster of leaves, usually at the base of a stem*
Sepal—*one unit of the calyx, usually green*
Serrate—*saw-toothed*
Sessile—*without a stalk, as in a leaf attached directly to the stem*
Sheath—*part of a leaf which folds about and encloses the stem*
Simple—*undivided leaf, as opposed to compound*
Spore—*usually one-celled asexual reproductive body, characteristic of ferns*
Succulent—*pulpy, juicy*
Taproot—*stout single main root, continuing down along the line of the stem*
Trifoliate—*having three leaflets*
Tuber—*short, thickened part of a rootstock*
Umbel—*flat-topped flower that looks like an umbrella*
Whorl—*three or more leaves or petals arranged in a circle*

INDEX

OTHER PACIFIC SEARCH BOOKS

THE GREEN TOMATO COOKBOOK *by Paula Simmons*

When you think "green tomato," if the only recipes that come to mind are "relish" and "fried tomatoes," you need THE GREEN TOMATO COOKBOOK. Paula Simmons, who solved the "too much zucchini" problem in her best-selling THE ZUCCHINI COOKBOOK, has worked the same magic with green tomatoes. No longer will that bumper crop dismay you. You'll find so many imaginative uses in this book—cookies, pies, meat dishes, taco sauce—that you'll probably be picking your tomatoes green on purpose, just to try out the recipes.
In paperback, 96 pp. $2.95
ISBN 0-914718-08-8

THE ZUCCHINI COOKBOOK *by Paula Simmons*

For year round good eating—think zucchini! Whether you grow it or buy it, if you think it can only be served one way, you need THE ZUCCHINI COOKBOOK, with over 100 tasty recipes, some created especially for the king-size zucchini. Recipes, written in a new, more readable style, run the gamut of kitchen artistry from irresistible chocolate zucchini cake and meringue zucchini pie to zucchini tetrazzini, and beer-battered blossoms. A longtime interest in creating and swapping recipes with other home gardeners led Paula Simmons to write this book.
In paperback, 128 pp. $3.50
ISBN 0-914718-05-3

WILD MUSHROOM RECIPES *by The Puget Sound Mycological Society*

For you who enjoy the pleasure of the search, the serendipity of discovery, the gourmet dreams of the sweet, succulent fruits of the earth. These are the special kinds of delight promised by this book. Wild mushrooms are the key but these imaginative recipes give the cultivated variety a special elegance as well. New second edition of over 200 recipes compiled by the field hunters and gourmet cooks of the Society.
In paperback, 178 pp. $6.95
ISBN 0-914718-04-5